HONEY, I WRECKED THE KIDS

When Yelling, Screaming, Threats, Bribes, Time-outs, Sticker Charts and Removing Privileges All Don't Work

ALYSON SCHAFER

Published by Collins, an imprint of HarperCollins Publishers Ltd

Originally published by John Wiley & Sons Canada, Ltd.: 2012
First published by HarperCollins Publishers Ltd in an EPub edition: 2013
This Collins trade paperback edition: 2014

HarperCollins books may be purchased for educational, business, or sales promo-
tional use through our Special Markets Department.

HarperCollins Publishers Ltd
2 Bloor Street East, 20th Floor
Toronto, Ontario, Canada
M4W 1A8

www.harpercollins.ca

Library and Archives Canada Cataloguing in Publication
information is available upon request.

ISBN 978-1-44342-778-4

Printed and bound in the United States of America
LSC 12 11

This book is dedicated to my dad, Richard (Dick) Knight. I owe him thanks for finding Adler's individual psychology, for teaching parent study groups in our living room, and for raising my brothers and me in a home that embraced social equality and democracy. His wisdom, character, and ideals helped shape me. Sadly, he passed away while I was still working on this second book. I know he was excited for me and eager to read it himself. Here it is, Dad. Better late than never, eh?

CONTENTS

ACKNOWLEDGMENTS

This book has been the result of many people's efforts, and I am grateful to the talent pool at Wiley Canada who all worked diligently on this project. Special thanks to Leah Fairbank, my editor, who always challenges me to do my best work and who twisted like a pretzel to keep this project moving during difficult circumstances.

I have been the beneficiary of so much. Everything I have written about comes from the philosophical tenets that Alfred Adler masterminded and that Dr. Rudolf Driekurs crafted into a child guidance system. I can take no credit for that, and yet, it's what makes the book powerful.

I also have learned from my many teachers, who must be acknowledged as well. Betty Lou Bettner's conceptualization of the 4 Crucial C's has changed the way I teach and speak on the four goals of misbehavior. Dr. Richard Royal Kopp taught me about the dynamics of power and how it plays out in families. These ideas are core to my work, and I thank these two dynamos for their brilliance.

Also, my heartfelt appreciation to my teachers who passed away this year: Dr. Oscar Christensen and Larry Nisan. These men taught me how to work with families by way of demonstration. It was always magical to watch both these gentle giants talk with children. Although they had very different styles, they could win the respect of children in mere moments. You know how they did it? They truly respected every child they met, and it was palpable in their dealings with them.

Last but far from least, there is my own family to thank. Ken, Zoe and Lucy are my strongest cheering section, and they carried the load for me when I needed to hunker down and write. They've told me to "pay-it-forward" to other families instead of re-paying my debt of time and attention to them. You guys rock!

INTRODUCTION
IT'S NEVER TOO LATE...

It's like most mornings. Coffee in hand, my dog follows me loyally to her spot under my desk. I settle in and open up my e-mail. And there it is again . . . like so many mornings. The subject line reads: HELP!!!

That HELP!!! is the digital siren call of yet another distraught parent who is at their wit's end, reaching out for advice on how to deal with a difficult child. They have no doubt already tried a litany of things to gain some control, and to regain peace and sanity. They have probably already read countless parenting books, tried the advice of a whole chorus of people (friends, family, other professionals), but they keep coming up short on finding *anything* that will work with their child. It seems there is a particular kind of child who just doesn't respond to the usual bag of tricks anymore. As I read on in this latest e-mail, I discover that sure enough, my hunches are correct. Here is some of what it says:

Alyson, I honestly could have had five kids if they were all like my eldest, Rebecca. But if we'd had Sam first, I swear we would have stopped at one child. One Sam is all we can handle—and frankly we aren't handling him well at all. If Rebecca misbehaved I would send her for a time-out and that was the end of it. No troubles—she's an angel child. But with Sam it is a totally different story. I tell him to go for a time-out and he looks me square in the eye and says "NO!" I literally have to go over and pick him up and carry him flailing in my arms. Even then he kicks and twists and hits my face! If I scold him and threaten to take away his Webkinz or TV time, he just LAUGHS like he couldn't care less—and truly, he doesn't. Help, Alyson. I love him and he is a sweet kid, but if this is what he is like at four, what will he be like at 14? Please HELP!

Do you have a "Sam" in your family—the kid who just doesn't respond to the old stand-by discipline techniques that work on other kids? Often it's not just a problem at home, but also at school. It can feel so public, and who wouldn't feel their parenting was coming under scrutiny?

So you spend your mornings wondering if there will be a phone call or note sent home again today. You sense the school is tiring of all the issues with your child, and the teacher says she has a class of 28 students and can't spend all her time dealing with yours. "It's not fair to the others." GULP. You're positive your child is becoming known as the "behavior case" in the staff room. Is she making a reputation for herself that she may never shake at the school? Should you just call ReMax now, list your home, get out of Dodge and start fresh where no one knows you. Then you remember she is only seven, and you can't be on the lamb for spitting. That's crazy talk. Or is it?

But maybe you're feeling a bit crazy yourself by now. Crazy, and most likely a little sorry for yourself, too. I can guess why. On top of the day-to-day problems, you also get none of the benefits other people seem to be enjoying with their children. Have you noticed how everyone else seems to look forward to family get-togethers, while you actually dread them? There are your brothers and sisters enjoying a Hallmark card moment with their children, but your fun is marred by your kid who generally puts a crimp in everything. Your sister is blissfully sipping her mojito and is free to indulge in adult-talk because her well-behaved children are off making their own fun, while you walk on eggshells hoping and praying that today your little piece of work will give it a rest, at least while the family is visiting. You can't bear to have them turn to you with that look of judgment. Frankly, you're starting to think that if you hear one more personal opinion mocking your inability to deal with your child YOU'LL be the behavior case!

People who don't have these issues with their children can't begin to imagine why you're having troubles. They can't appreciate your parenting stress: not your family, not your pediatrician, not even your pals in your moms' group. Your co-workers at the office don't have a clue how issues with a child can be so all-consuming. The ripple effects of having a discipline-resistant child in the family create a virtual tsunami of relationship breakdowns: siblings create and break alliances, and Mom and Dad find themselves at war over how best to deal with the call that just came in from the neighbor (please, no ... not another after-school "incident"). Worse, the stress of non-stop damage control can begin to unravel marriages. Short tempers lead to resentments; then come the potshots and worse:

"Oh pleaaaase just shut up and let me handle this!"
"Well, if you would just try it my way for a change!"
"You're as pigheaded as her. . . ."

Cutting remarks, tearing each other down, feeling unheard, disrespected, unsupported, challenged. . . . It sure isn't what you thought family life was going to be when you were sipping tea and rubbing your pregnant belly while wearing hubby's big wool socks. Starting a family was supposed to make your love grow! Instead you're sure this kid is going to ruin your marriage and hinder or harm the siblings who (touch wood) don't act like this.

On top of losing a sense of connection with your own family, you can begin to feel like a social pariah. There is a zero-tolerance policy for other parents' misbehaving kids, if you haven't already noticed. The parents of discipline-resistant children tell me they feel like modern-day lepers. No one wants your child to "rub off" on *their* precious darlings. What happened to a collegial "not to worry, boys will be boys"? No, instead you watch as the other parents—sitting in their tribal circles of folding camp chairs along the soccer sidelines—talk among themselves. And you, in your growing paranoia, swear you overheard them say you must be grooming the next Unabomber.

I work with many parents who are at their wit's end, trying to deal with one or more of their children who just doesn't respond to traditional parenting. The old standards like time-outs or taking away privileges (ah—thanks Dr. Phil, but that didn't work either), the things you see other parents doing, even the things you know worked with your other children, NONE of it makes a difference, not with your discipline-resistant child. Grrrrr!

Sam and Rebecca's parents, the couple who e-mailed me, have been suffering alone, feeling like they are a parenting anomaly. Actually, their family situation isn't unusual at all. The discipline-resistant child is now a common phenomenon: kids who won't listen, won't do as they're told, refuse to sit still in their seat at school or keep to their curfew. They don't think the rules apply to them, and these children aren't an oddity or a rare case study—they are everywhere!

Sometime between removing the door so he couldn't slam it anymore and pushing his shelf into the hall so he couldn't chuck storybooks at me when I sent him to his room, I thought to myself—this is crazy. We can't go on forever disassembling the house—I need help.

These pleas for help are not just a matter of reaching out for new discipline techniques; they are also about addressing the common fear that—just maybe—our parenting practices are actually making matters worse. Could it be that we as parents are the source of this new modern phenomenon, the evolution of an actual "Discipline-Resistant Child?" These kids are like those super bugs that doctors warn you about: antibiotic-resistant strains of bacteria that have become resistant to any form of intervention. In fact, the very medicine that was supposed to be a cure instead made the bugs even stronger. They're actually MORE virulent and wreak total havoc now that nothing can stop them.

Hmmm . . . does that sound a lot like what's happened with the kids? Parents send me e-mails all in bold caps written at 3 a.m.:

It's my fault! Could all those threats and scoldings and all those failed discipline attempts actually have contributed to the problems I am seeing in my child? Is this because I was too inconsistent? Was it my anger? Was I overly harsh? Too lenient? Impatient? Did I actually contribute to building this difficult child?? HELP! What the HELL am I doing?

I can imagine their heads hitting the desk when they finish writing, then crawling back to bed where their partner asks, "Everything alright?"

"Honey, I wrecked the kids!"

If this sounds like you, then I am glad you found this book. When I work with families like yours, I actually get energized and excited because I know that the situation can be turned around. In fact, I have worked through this process with enough families that I am eager to begin the revolution. I know that there are "ah-ha" moments and great relief just ahead.

This generation of children behaves in a way that burdens us all, and it's time that we addressed the situation properly instead of blaming parents and slapping around diagnoses like "conduct disorder" or "oppositional-defiant disorder." In this book, I will dig deeply to tell a much broader story of human nature. I will talk about what motivates behaviors, both good and bad, and include parents' behavior, too.

Think of this book as the "owner's manual" we keep saying kids don't come with. I will take the time to lay the foundation so you can understand your difficult child and then learn how to parent effectively.

Every parent can benefit from having a larger framework for understanding his or her child's behavior, so that when you read articles online, in magazines, or watch shows on TV you'll be capable of evaluating the advice. It will become much easier for you to decide if you want to integrate or disregard the barrage of information that will continue to come your way. I offer you a considered parenting model that is both theoretical and philosophical, but that also cuts through the rhetoric to give you pragmatic techniques and strategies.

So if you are willing to bring an open mind and let me poke you in the ribs to keep you laughing through this, I promise to show you a better life with your child. I will teach you how to analyze the situations that are going awry through a whole bunch of hauntingly familiar examples. And, yes, to answer your question, I do sometimes spy in your windows at night to collect these stories! You'll begin to see the patterns that are your nemesis and learn new ways to handle them with your discipline-resistant child.

In the pages ahead, I'm also going to show you the most common pitfalls, stumbling blocks and traps that get in the way of effective parenting. Some of you will recognize these right away, and realize that you have already started on the right track—you just need to make some subtle changes to carry through.

The first step is to commit to getting to the heart of the issues instead of concerning ourselves with the simplistic and superficial eradication of behavioral symptoms. Quick-fix solutions don't hold up in the long run. The answers lie in understanding human dynamics.

Did you ever take psychology courses? Do you remember learning about Alfred Adler, Sigmund Freud and Carl Jung? These men were the triumvirate that really cracked open modern psychology. They were intellectual sparring partners and they moved each other's theories forward. They developed, in concert, an idea of human personality development that is known as the "psychodynamic perspective." It is the foundational roots from which nearly all systems of family counseling and family therapy are derived.

My Master's degree is from the Adler School in Chicago. My professional training is in Adlerian family counseling and parenting, and I was raised by parents who had studied and taught Adlerian theory. My father and grandmother founded the Alfred Adler Institute of Ontario. In fact, my grandmother was the first dean. So, yes, I admit it, I had a *slight* leaning to this approach. Growing up, I knew my family home was different than my friends', and I was glad.

But I also chose to study Adler because I wanted to work with children and their families, and Adler's greatest contribution was a form of child guidance practices that were based on principles of respect and dignity. Adler was fixated with the idea of human co-operation, a seemingly simplistic and yet ever elusive idea. His ideas have been proven effective in many studies from various fields, and they are just now really catching the attention of the masses.

Adler was a recognized master for working therapeutically with troubled children. Parents who have discipline-resistant children and who feel that they have tried everything have not yet been introduced to his ideas and methods. But these ideas are fundamental to the changes we must implement in order to effectively parent this new generation.

So can we change our children's behavior? Is it too late? Did we wreck the kids? Of course not! The beauty of human beings is that they can change. That is why I am a therapist. That is why you don't read signs at the clinic door saying, "Clients over five years old not accepted—no chance of change."

This morning, with my dog still at my feet, I've decided that rather than sending one e-mail back to my most recent cry for HELP!!! I'm going to write a much longer response—this book. It's not just for Sam's parents, but for anyone who needs help, and especially for anyone who is ready for change.

Discipline-resistant kids who are driving us crazy and testing every boundary they can find are actually our nation's most precious resource. They are the people who are going to drive our future, by hook or by crook, and they are banging on our doors: Wake up! We want change!

Let the revolution begin . . . .

CHAPTER ONE
THE SOLUTION

Yes, there *is* a social revolution underfoot in your living room. It's an unconventional battleground to be sure. We're caught in one-on-one combat with our children in so many homes across the nation that no one notices the huge number of causalities this inter-generational war is creating. As dramatic as that all sounds, I actually think this is an exciting time and, frankly, I believe it will prove to be as historically important a time as the civil rights movement or our bra burning feminist foremothers' campaign for women's rights.

• •

History was never made by anyone who was obedient.

• •

THE PROBLEM
Now we are experiencing the "children's revolution" . . . and if you have a child who is locking horns with your parental authority, you've got yourself a freedom fighter, a real Rosa Parks. Today's children are

letting us know with their behaviors that our current discouraging ways of parenting can't continue. I say *hurray*!

Many kids just can't be made to mind anymore. You tell them, "It's time to practice piano," and they refuse. You say, "Stop running!" They don't. You ask them to close the fridge door, and they roll their eyes and keep gazing trance-like at its mundane contents.

In short, they are disobedient (and that is just the *first* thing I like about these kids). It reminds me of my own rebel mom, who fought for the right to wear pants as an elementary teacher in the '60s. Doesn't a "no pants" rule for women sound barbaric now? "The times they are a changin'" and it's all for the better, even if change seems scary right now.

Today's enlightened parents get that. I talk with them all the time. They tell me they don't want to be discouraging. In fact, they really are motivated to be great parents, and to do right by their kids. They want their children to be treated respectfully, to grow to be their own people. They want to parent in a way that helps their child self-actualize into their full potential. Ahhhhh—what a nice ambition. Probably an idea you came up with when you were smitten with your swaddled babe and still high on being a new parent, but as time passed those sentiments turned into:

> *Alyson, I hope you can help me. My son Jasper is four years old and we are getting into a lot of situations that I don't know how to handle. He really should know better by now. Like when we go to swimming lessons, he won't get out of the pool, he acts all silly and won't get his clothes on, choosing instead to dance around and make faces into the mirror. I end up losing it each time: I finally snap. Why can't he just listen?*

Two Approaches to a Familiar Problem

Well, this is where the rubber hits the road. All our great parenting ideals about how we're not going to squelch our child's self-esteem come to a crashing halt when our armpits are dripping in sweat from chasing our naked monkey-child through a steamy change room at the public pool. What are we supposed to do now?

Parents in change rooms all over the nation just throw their hands in the air and ponder the cosmic question, "Why can't they just listen?" Why can't *all* these kids just listen? We could put an end to *all* this misery if our kids would just LISTEN.

But I ask you, really, isn't that just another way of saying we simply wish they'd be obedient? Yes, you read that correctly. I said *obedient*. I am asking you very seriously, how does that sound to you? Would you like to have an obedient child—is that *your solution*?

There seem to be two reactions to that question. One camp of parents shout proudly: "Damn right! Children should be obedient. After all, I am the grown-up and they are only children who don't know what they are doing. They need to respect their elders and listen to the rules. We make these rules for their own good. It's okay if they don't like it. Tough! I was raised this way and I turned out fine."

If that sounds something like your line of thinking, then you fall into a camp of parents whose numbers are vast. For centuries this has been the outlook of parents. It is our cultural history to parent in this autocratic style. Parents hold the power, children are made to be obedient underlings, and behavior is controlled or manipulated by the use of punishment and rewards to keep children in line. That's it in a nutshell, and we've been doing it pretty much this way since the Middle Ages.

But there is also an opposing camp of parents. They have totally rejected our past parenting traditions, feeling they are too disrespectful to children. If your response to the word *obedient* was "Yuck, I don't want to raise some patsy child who is blindly obedient," then you'll feel at home with another full camp of like-minded parents. Raising an "obedient child" sounds too militaristic for this generation of soya slugging, eco-conscious, blogger mommies. *Hello*—obedient? Are you kidding? They abhor the idea; these parents are too rebellious themselves. They remember the totalitarian regime of their own childhoods, and don't want to repeat it for their children.

This group of parents is a formidable force today and growing in numbers all the time. They even look to bona fide research to support their arguments. They have read up on early brain growth, attachment patterns and the importance of positive parental bonding experiences. They zealously reject the old cultural model of "father knows best," and instead focus on "what's best for the babe." Their reading has left them fearful about the fragility of their children's psyches. They worry any negative emotions or psychological struggles might be damaging. The result is that these ambitious, nervous parents become "helicopter parents" that hover, protect, overdo, do for and generally intercede and rescue their children from life's distresses. This is the "pampering" or "permissive" group of parents.

Most parents identify, at least loosely, with one of these two camps or attitudinal outlooks, and each tends to loathe the ways of the other. The autocrats think pampering parents should just get a grip, grab the reins and get their wild children under control, while the pampering parents think the autocrats are old school, disrespectful of their children's rights and controlling. What neither camp realizes is that on closer inspection, they have more in common than meets the eye.

Let's check back in with Mom at the swimming pool. Which camp do you think she is in? After asking Jasper the monkey-man nicely to "Please help Mommy by getting your pants on," and after Jasper completely ignores his mother's gentle, respectful request for the ump-teenth time, she grows angry that her respectfulness is not being recip-rocated in kind. She thinks to herself "Hey, come on man, I am being a nice mommy; where's the co-operation you owe me for asking you nicely? Why aren't you thankful and appreciative? You have this nice loving respectful mommy, so why won't you listen to me and get your #%$^*&^* pants on!" Bewildered and bankrupt of ideas for what else to do, she defaults to "If you don't get your pants on this INSTANT . . ." raising her voice and uttering threats.

She wants to go the respectful route, but when her back is up against the wall, she defaults to punitive measures or bribes. The autocrats and the pamperers use the same techniques—only the pam-pering parents feel bad about it, while the autocrats feel justified.

And so it goes, all over the nation, parents oscillating between asking for co-operation, and when that fails, returning to punitive measures.

These two camps of parents are really just two sides of the same coin. It's like watching the proverbial Slave and Tyrant Show. In the autocratic household, it's clear the parent is the tyrant and the child is the slave. In the pampering and permissive home, the parents have abdicated their position on the throne, believing it will put an end to the tyranny, only to realize that their child has discovered the vacant throne and jumped right in. "Get me a grill cheese; I am NOT eating that ham," they proclaim. "Yes, your highness, coming right up. After all, you must eat some protein today," the permissive parent dutifully replies.

Parents take this abuse for a while, and after sufficient feelings of oppression, the pampering parent rises up and the roles reverse temporarily, yet again. "Hey, you're playing me, aren't you? I thought you really didn't like ham, but your teachers say you eat it at daycare!

I am not your short-order cook. Eat the ham or go hungry. (Well, but don't starve. If you're really hungry, I'll get you a yogurt tube later, babe.)"

This is crazy-making!

If we look back over our history, we'd realize this child revolution was imminent. In cases of civil unrest, the oppressed eventually rally and overthrow their oppressors. Sadly, history also teaches us that once the oppressed get into power, they seem to immediately have some kind of massive amnesia attack and merrily go on to repeat the abuses on others that they themselves just fought to be free of.

How can people learn to get along without dominating and oppressing? How do we co-operate instead of compete with one another? As if those aren't hard enough questions: How do you both co-operate AND be the disciplinarian to a three-year-old who wants to eat Play-Doh and jump on the couch? It's a brain twister, isn't it? But there is a solution.

An Alternative Solution

In my first book, *Breaking the Good Mom Myth*, I revealed to "do-gooder mothers" that we're living in toxic times for family life but we don't notice it because we're so busy keeping up with the maladjusted Joneses. Most of what we embraced as parenting "best practices" are actually "worst practices."

In this book I promise to show you another way and give you the tools to change your family life forever. I am going to teach you that elusive third choice for parenting. This is not some diluted auto-cratic system that's been injected with warm fuzzies to help with PR problems. And, no, it is not a "pumped-up" pampering system that has undergone assertiveness training to try to give it some backbone. This is a totally different parenting model: it's like switching from a PC to a Mac. This is a different operating system, a different view of children, how to motivate them, guide them and how to correct their behaviors. It's the peaceful solution to the child revolution.

What is the solution then? An equitable process known as "Democratic Parenting." It leads to truly co-operative families that thrive together and support one another. It's not just a wish—it's a full-parenting plan that comes with a blueprint to follow and a ton of techniques to learn. Given that the family is the basic social building block for a harmonious society, efforts to improve our families by raising co-operative children are the tickets to moving us closer to a less conflict-divided world. Lofty stuff, hey?

Welcome to Democratic Parenting

Democratic Parenting is the solution and we are the early adopters. Welcome! I am so glad you found us. This book is about new-era discipline. I've got tons of practical help for how to pull this off in real life. Every week I teach and coach parents how to implement these ideas in their lives. I am familiar with where concepts are most easily misapplied or tripped up, and I will warn you about the traps children set that we parents often get caught in. I can speak to all of these issues as we go along and help you stay the course. Now, are you getting excited about the change that is coming your way? I hope so. If not—no worries. I am excited enough for both of us.

Why Obedience Sucks

Let me make sure you have a complete grasp of the obedience model so you are able to loathe it as much as I do, since I am putting forth an argument that makes the desire (hidden or overt) for having an obedient child as unthinkable and crazy-sounding as installing a coal-burning stove or leaving on all the lights in your house.

We tend to define obedience simply as obeying authority, and we interpret that to mean "listen to your parents" (which does sound innocent enough). But training our children to be obedient and to always listen to their parents and other authorities has substantive pitfalls that I want to make you aware of. Here are some questions to ask yourself:

1. What if an authority is not well-meaning?
2. How will your children learn to evaluate situations and make good judgments?
3. How does being punished and rewarded affect your children in the long run?

Let's examine each of these questions:

What If an Authority Is Not Well-Meaning?

I, for one, want my children to challenge the cultural imperative that we *must* respect our elders. I say "pshaw." What are we, a bunch of ageists? When did the mere fact of being an elder guarantee your respectability? I can think of all kinds of adults I don't want my child to listen to. The Rev. Jim Jones and pimps come to mind. But more realistically, it's the seemingly benign uncle or trusted clergyman we need to worry about. There is an implicit belief that other adults always have our child's best interests at heart. But sadly, it's just not true, and we can't afford to be wrong.

In most every case of childhood sexual abuse, the pedophile was a trusted authority figure, and they sought the obedient child, trained to submit. Obedience leaves our youngsters unprotected from dangerous adults.

That is something to remember the next time you urge your child to eat with the ole' "Come on honey, just o-o-o-ne more bite of chicken for mommy." This may seem innocent, but when we do this, we inadvertently teach our children to ignore and stifle their inner voice that is saying "No!"

I want my children to learn to listen to that little voice inside that feels uncomfortable, and I also want them to feel confident enough to honor those feelings and empowered enough to speak up and say "NO" to another person—regardless of their age.

Remember, too, that the sweet tot who listens so dutifully to you in their childhood will eventually become a teenager. When their gonads start to mature and suddenly your house reeks of AXE (the body spray that puts the "scent" in pubescent), your obedient teen will switch allegiance from parents to peers as the new authority.

You might have said, "Get in your car seat," and expected no push-back from your preschooler, but fast-forward 12 years, and now it's your daughter's boyfriend, only he is asking her to get in the *back* seat. Don't you wish she would say no now? If she is a good obedient girl, she stands less of a chance. She is out to please authority, and while once it was *you* she wanted to please, now it's her boyfriend and her clique of girlfriends.

How Will Your Children Learn to Evaluate Situations and Make Good Judgments?

With an obedience model, the child (or any subservient for that matter) is asked NOT to think for themselves. After all, that might stir up dissent. Instead, they are trained to simply follow orders without thought, comprehension or agreement. That can make for easy work in the beginning. This strategy is a good "quick fix," but a short-sighted approach. And sure, some children even *like* being told what to do. It's a low-risk endeavor, if you're willing to submit. No fear of making a mistake if you're just following orders from someone else. "Don't blame me; he said so." "Don't look at me; I didn't decide." Low responsibility is a nice little insurance plan for those who fear making mistakes and potentially looking bad. Many children do, but at what cost?

The child who has been trained to look outside herself, to seek an external authority for answers, is developing a life handicap. How will she fare when no authority is available? The simple question, "What do *you* want?" becomes unbearable for the middle-aged woman in therapy who has spent a lifetime pleasing her parents, her husband, her boss, her children. "I don't know what I want!" she cries out. "I don't know who I am!"

The idea of working with our children to help them develop their own compass to guide them is a much more sound pursuit, don't you think?

How Does Being Punished and Rewarded Affect Your Children in the Long Run?

Usually one of your children will be a willing subservient, the "compliant child," and the other will not. (I'll tell you more about why that is in an upcoming chapter.) If you don't have a willing subservient, you have to rely on the use of punishments and rewards to produce the compliance and behaviors you want. These are the tools of obedience. The person in the superior position of power is the authority and the underlings must submit their personal power. Why do they submit? They either really want that sticker you're luring them with (and the love and acceptance that it symbolizes), or they act out of fear. They're sure not acting out of their own self-determination or desire to be helpful. They're snared into a course of action. Remove the snare and the behavior goes with it. The teacher leaves the room; the obedient children go wild in celebration of freedom from supervision.

We know definitively from research that the use of rewards is de-motivating to children, so if you think paying them to keep their room clean is a good tactic—think again. When they can earn minimum wage working at the mall, they won't clean their room for love nor money. And if you offer a $2 reward for keeping their room clean each week, don't be appalled when you ask them to help unload groceries and they answer, "For how much?" We teach them free market economy instead of co-operation.

If, on the other hand, you are cheap and don't like doling out the reward, you can always go with the other tool—punishment. Then you are relying on fear as a motivator. Do you want your children to fear you? They will. But children who live in fear are not free to fully develop themselves. They can't reach their full potential when they worry about pain and getting hurt. Of course they would take the safe route. Who would risk a potential mistake when upsetting parents leads to suffering?

Punishment hurts the relationship and the intimacy bond between parent and child. It's twisted to think people who love you will also purposefully hurt you. How will that manifest in their future love relationships? Do you replace a punishing parent with an abusive spouse? Some children come to believe they deserve this treatment. That breaks my heart. And even if they have a healthy self-esteem, they aren't stupid. Would you tell a punishing parent that you think you left your Nintendo DS at the hockey arena? NO way! Much better to lie and evade a certain punishment.

If our children think, "I must do what I am told, or I'll be punished," then imagine how that will play out with our previous example of the teens who look to their peers as their authority. Our obedient teen daughters will believe, "If I don't get in the back seat with my boyfriend, he'll break up with me and find a girl who will, and my social status will plummet." Our daughters will fear they will slide down some imaginary merit scale. Whether a cheerleader type, the athletic girl, the beauty queen, the academic or the alt-geek, there is a misguided social status scale that is metaphysical and yet as orienting as the meridian lines on the globe. We want our kids to be ready to face these pressures!

The notion that some people are better and above others is just distasteful, isn't it? Jocks are no better than geeks. How did our teens become so misguided? Hmmm, could it be that we inadvertently taught them this scale from a very young age when we demanded them to submit to us, arguing we are their "superiors"? But, adults are not "superior" to children, just as whites are no better than blacks, and Christians are not a "better people" than Jews.

There is *no status scale* to climb or slide down. Not for our daughter in the back seat, not for us as struggling parents worried about being judged by other mommies with "well-behaved" children. Not for anyone. Instead we are all on the even footing called "humanity," and we face the challenge of how to live side by side rather than one-up, one-down.

I hope I have made you feel uncomfortable with the notion of having obedient children. I also want to be your guide as you commit to the elimination of punishment and rewards in our homes, so that you don't take that predictable backslide into pampering when you feel helpless with disciplining your child effectively.

The democratic model will require new tools and protocols: it requires a shift in the way we view children and our typical dealings with them. The old tapes in our heads need to be replaced with new ones. It's all doable—and it's all worth it. Frankly, it's unstoppable, so get on the ride and enjoy it instead of fighting it. It's the 21st century, and it's critical we learn to live co-operatively on a global as well as a personal level if we are to survive.

Let's forgo domination and submission, punishment and rewards and all the other trappings required to raise obedient children. Instead, let's put our sights on a more worthy goal and a far grander pursuit: to raise a truly co-operative child.

To do so, we must accept the egalitarian nature of humanity with no woman, man or child ruling over another. We are meant to work together; not to compete, and not to conquer and divide, so we need both parent and child to abdicate the position of "ruler over others" in the family. Instead we must be willing to work together to build a family that supports all of its members. Kids raised in this manner will be well-equipped to be leaders of own their own lives, and also leaders for their whole generation. Isn't that what we had hoped for? It's an inspiring parenting goal, and it is in reach.

CHAPTER TWO
COW IN A PARTY DRESS

So we begin the journey into becoming a democratic family. I know that many of you reading this book may already be suffering "parenting fatigue" from all the efforts you've made before picking up this book. I have given you my promise that I will point out the pitfalls that trip parents up, so that this time you will get progress for your efforts. And, true to my word, here is the first:

Watch out for the cow in a party dress.

A bovine in a frock ain't fooling anybody, and likewise, you are going to look just as foolish to your children if you only "try on" some of this democratic parenting stuff for size. I want you to find success in the pages ahead, but to really pull this off and bring about the desired change in your family life, there has to be a change from within, a new worldview. It's about adopting a stance so that your intentions are genuine when you carry out your parenting actions.

This is when you'll really notice that your new efforts are proving effective. Yes, you can "fake it till you make it," and, yes, all the new skills you'll be learning do take some time and practice before competency develops, but underneath all that, there must be a first-order change in your desired aims and goals. It's like developing a yoga practice. You can't just buy a Lululemon outfit and drop in on a class now and then. I am asking you to commit to "developing your parenting practice."

That's where my job as author and therapist kicks in. I have the auspicious charge of helping you to have some ah-ha moments, what we in the psyche biz call "cognitive reframes." These are new ways of understanding, in this case, new ways of seeing our "misbehaving" children.

I want to show you a fresh perspective on your children and their behaviors that will help you deepen your desires to adopt these approaches, to pull them off with real heart, and to see your children in a positive light, believing in their capacities for change and co-operation. New information should help shape your lens and perceptions such that you have a new take on the problems you're encountering, and can believe more firmly in the solutions you'll be committed to applying. Here is the plan for change:

Change parental attitudes
(from gleaning new information in this book)

Results in authentic changes in parental behavior
(using these pragmatic techniques)

Change in parent-child relationship
(MAGICAL MOMENTS AHEAD!)

Change in child's attitudes and beliefs
(You've influenced how they perceive themselves—bravo!)

Change in child's behavior!!!
(New actions follow new beliefs—co-operation!)

WHY THE BEHAVIORIST MODEL DOESN'T WORK

Notice there are a few more steps than the behaviorist approach everyone seems so quick to accept. It's hard to fathom that with such popularity, longevity and widespread appeal the behaviorist approach could actually be an ineffective course of action. Well, hey, it wouldn't be the first time something popular and well-accepted went without being challenged, only later to be debunked; the canon of needing to drink eight glasses of water a day, the benefits of frontal lobotomies and asbestos insulation have all gone the way of the hula hoop.

The problem with the popular behaviorist approach is that it only tackles change at the bottom of the change cascade. It identifies only the child's behavior as being problematic. It ignores any internal thoughts, perceptions, social or relational issues that give rise to their choice of actions. It merely seeks to alter the end result: behaviors. But, because the behaviorist approach is simple and measurable, it sure does look mighty attractive to parents and teachers. No wonder it's so wildly popular. It relieves the adult of any responsibility to address the deeper issues and also to change themselves. Only the child is seen as being "wrong" and "in need of fixing."

It's a faulty approach. Why? Because humans are complex. It's the price we pay for having an opposable thumb and a huge prefrontal cortex.

Maybe you've experienced a "behavioral belly flop" first hand in your own life. Have you ever tried to do something as "simple and measurable" as losing weight? Just eat less and the scale will drop, right? Gosh, what is so hard about that? Maybe your spouse even said you could have a new wardrobe or some other token reward if you lost the extra pounds you've been packing on since the baby came along. How could you go wrong with that offer? Yet, time and time again we are met with failure to change our behaviors (to the tune of a billion-dollar-a-year diet industry). It just isn't as simple as we want to believe it is.

There are body image issues, social customs, food triggers, emotional eating, bad habits, stress issues and so on. No surprise that stomach stapling, wiring jaws, and other "simple" behavioral fixes don't work long term. Bribing Evan by telling him that you'll take him bowling if he has a "good week at school and listens to Miss Kendall" is about as likely to work as telling Mama Cass to just back away from the Twinkie.

CHANGING PERCEPTIONS: FROM PROBLEM TO PROMISING

Another very difficult thing to change is parents' preconceived notions about their children. It is undeniable that children will move in line with parental expectations. Children are young and quickly adaptable: they change their ways very quickly. What is far, far harder, in my practice, is changing the parents' expectations about their so-called problem child.

If you continue to think about Derrick as the Freddie Kreuger of the family, I promise he won't disappoint. The situation will not change no matter how many techniques Derrick's parents apply from this book. We *must* start seeing our difficult children in a positive way if we want to see them act in a positive way.

That means we need to start by coming to terms with what their misbehavior is really all about. After all, it's their choice of behaviors that are devilish, not themselves. Why is that important? Because a child can change her behaviors, but she can't change who she is. Never forget that. Separate the deed from the doer. Children can always do different deeds. Change is always possible. Always. Every day we get a new chance. Everything can be different. Hallelujah!

Understanding Children's Misbehavior

So why *do* children do what they do? Why do they get in trouble? Why does Jamie hit his sister when he knows he will be punished? How come he can't see that his life would be so much easier if he would just keep his hands to himself? Why does this elude him? It's like he *wants* to makes his own life hell. Mind-boggling, isn't it?

Jamie's motives and actions don't make any sense to his parents. But they do to Jamie, or else he wouldn't have any reason to keep it up! Unfortunately, Jamie's motives are pre-conscious, so it's not like we can just ask him. That means from now on, we can strike these infamous parenting lines from our repertoire: "Why did you do that?" and "What were you thinking?"

• •

Bogus Parenting Lines to Drop Right Now

"Why did you do that?"
"What were you thinking?"
"Go to your room and think about what you did."
"You've got some explaining to do, mister."
"I swear I don't know what you are thinking half the time!"

• •

Children are not trying to evade your question when they look blankly at you and answer "I dunno," or worse, when they make something up to get you to stop interrogating them, only to then be accused of lying too. Children trying to answer these questions often just deduce, "I don't know why I do bad things; I guess it's because I am a bad person."

Ouch, that's gotta hurt.

In reality, Jamie (and all people for that matter) is simply incapable of accessing pre-conscious information, and that is where the answer resides in the brain. We can't fault people for that. We need to either bring the information into the conscious part of the brain, or we need to find the answers through a means *other* than direct confrontation.

• •

New Insight #1: Children don't know WHY they misbehave—it's pre-conscious.

• •

Let me share what I know about the "why" of misbehavior so you can learn to decipher what's going on for yourself. Why does Liam pitch a fit when you have the audacity to pull his stuck sock off (when he wanted to do it by himself)? And how can it be that the fit continues, even when you offer to put the sock *back* on his foot. No use! He's off to tantrum land again, kicking you with the sockless foot in question.

What do you think? Is Liam being "unreasonably emotional"? Is he "out to get you" in some way? Is he acting "out of line"? These thoughts will naturally take you back to the old way of dealing with children that says, "Better teach him a lesson, and show him his place."

However, if we see Liam's tantrum for what it *really* is, if we interpret the situation differently, we'll find it far more easy and inviting to respond in democratic ways.

It's the same process that would happen if you learned that the reason your dog started nipping at you is NOT because he suddenly doesn't like you or because he was becoming a mean dog, but rather because he has a thorn in his paw and he doesn't want you to touch it. Understanding that situation from a new perspective allows you to find empathy, and then you can choose to go about doing things a different way. Now you work to remove the thorn instead of scowling back at his nipping behavior. You treat the dog as one that is hurting, not one that is "bad." I want you to accomplish that same adjustment in thinking about your children who are giving you grief, but without pitying or pampering.

Misbehavior Is a Misnomer

The first thing to get your head around is the idea that misbehavior is just a negative label. It's kind of like weeds; the only thing that makes a plant a weed is that it's not wanted. So too with children's behavior.

"Misbehavior" is a term that is exclusively adult-to-child language and it is tied to the way in which adults have traditionally viewed children.

We need to step outside of our traditional adult-centric perspective and get inside the world of the child for a moment. Children experiment with different behaviors, trying out different ways of acting as they grow and navigate life. They go about this by observing, imitating and emulating others, especially their parents. Beyond imitation and emulation, children also make good use of their own inventiveness and creativity, coming up with new behaviors. Who they choose to emulate, and which behaviors they get drawn to is their own personal decision. That means you can't blame big brother for setting a bad example or point the finger at that little putz Randall down the street who you think is a bad influence. Other children's behaviors don't "rub off" passively like dust or get transmitted like lice, as we seem to think. It may be pre-conscious, but behaviors are always of one's own choosing.

When deciding how to behave, kids observe how others respond to them when they act in a variety of ways. Based on experimentation and the process of trial and error, children deem their actions to be either "effective" or "ineffective" depending on the social responses they get from others.

That is very different than the adult interpretation of children being "good" or "bad," as if there were some moral matter at hand. There just isn't. It only makes sense that if a child discovers that a behavior gets a desired social response, then the child also learns that the behavior is effective. So, why not repeat it? Go with what you know works. Brilliant!

Alternately, if it isn't working—don't bother. Why waste the energy? Best to drop the ineffective behaviors from the repertoire. So if your eight-year-old is still pooping his pants, you can cancel the exorcism. He is not wrecked or possessed—just bright and creative, and it would seem that he benefits in some way from your reactions to crapping his pants, strange as that may seem.

Children's behavior is their creative attempt at getting some of their needs met. Instead of thinking of them as misbehaving *per se*, think of them as simply using a mistaken approach to get their needs met. They have lit upon an effective behavior that works for them, but it's bothering us! Our job as parents is to help them get what they need through alternate means.

Now this is shaping up into a new way of thinking about your misbehaving child.

New Insight #2: Misbehavior is really just a mistaken approach.

Of course, it begs the question, what exactly are these so-called needs that children feel are not being met? Let's look.

What Do Children Need?

It turns out that all men, women and children are striving to fulfill four essential needs for their own mental well-being. I bet you don't know what they are. Funny that, hey?

We probably all know what we need for physical health, but what about mental well-being? Nope. We often don't know where to begin conceptualizing that. With physical health it's all about nutrition, being active, getting proper sleep and whatnot. Every woman's magazine is chock full of this stuff. Yet, as a society, we largely ignore the requirements for good mental health.

Here are the four needs that every person has:

- The need to feel **connected**: I need to believe I am accepted and that I belong.
- The need to feel **capable**: I need to believe I can do it! That I am competent and can manage.
- The need to feel **counted**: I need to believe I count for something, that my contributions make a difference.
- The need to feel **courageous**: I need to believe I can handle what comes.

Betty Lou Bettner, PhD and author of *Raising Kids Who Can*, created this easy-to-remember formula and calls these "The 4 Crucial C's." From birth to death, we all seek in different ways to continually fulfill these human needs. A person who fulfills all these Crucial C's will be a mentally healthy and happy person who is resilient and functions well in their interpersonal relationships. Now imagine if these Crucial C's were not fulfilled. What if some of the Crucial C's were lacking?

Deficiency in the 4 Crucial C's

- I don't feel I am accepted or belong; I feel insecure, isolated, lonely and marginalized.
- I don't feel I am capable; I feel incompetent, powerless and dependent.
- I don't feel I count or have any value; I feel worthless and insignificant.
- I don't feel courageous, I can't manage life's problems; I feel I am not okay because I am not perfect.

A person who feels isolated, powerless, worthless and fearful is fraught with feelings of inferiority. He or she will struggle to overcome these feelings. It's in the struggle to overcome these feelings and perceived deficiencies that people conduct themselves negatively, aggressively and generally in very different ways than the "C positive" people who feel connected, capable, counted and courageous.

Lacking in any of the 4 Crucial C's results in feelings of discouragement, and misbehavior is *always* the result of feeling discouraged.

. . . .

New Insight #3: Misbehaviors are our children's response to feeling discouraged.

. . . .

The greater the discouragement, the greater the struggle to compensate for it. If you have ever flubbed a job interview or made an ass of yourself on a first date, you know that when we question ourselves, when we feel small and awkward, we don't act "naturally" at all. Frankly, we go all weird. Even if we are aware that it's happening, we seem incapable of stopping ourselves. For discouraged children, every day is one looooong first date that is going badly: it never ends!

For adults, these "missteps" can mean getting passed over for the job or not being asked out for the second date. For children, however, it usually results in being punished for "not behaving." That punishment creates more feelings of inferiority, not belonging, being powerless and not counting. And so the cycle spirals downward to more struggles and worse behaviors, leading to worse punishment.

• •

Kids who feel good—do good. Kids who feel bad—do bad.
—Dr. Jane Nelson

• •

Thankfully, all children are born with the ambition to fulfill the Crucial C's. We don't need to motivate them: it's innate. No stickers required! But we do need to point them in the right direction, show them the way, and create experiences that help them get each of their needs fulfilled on the "positive side of life" through useful and co-operative methods. It is only if their efforts are thwarted, if they can't find a way to meet these needs through positive endeavors, then, and *only* then, do they work to get their needs met through negative means. Then the mistaken approaches appear.

There is a similar survival mechanism in embryonic development. I remember that when I was pregnant my doctor cautioned me that if I didn't drink enough milk to supply the needed calcium to the fetus through my diet, the baby would take the calcium from my bones. What a smart baby. Sure, the preference is from the proper source, namely, the food you eat, but failing that, babies will seek survival by looking for less optimal alternatives.

So, we are charged with the task of making sure we have a home life rich in all four of the Crucial C's. The democratic methods and tools you'll be learning will make your home "C positive." Currently, most of our home and school environments are leading to "C deficits" for children; consequently, misbehaviors abound. Let's look more closely at each one.

Connection—I Need to Believe I Belong

Will your children find belonging in the family, or seek out a different group who wants them?

Did you know that Canadian geese fly in a V-formation because this reduces the air drag by about 10 percent for each of them individually? They also rotate which bird is flying in point position, so no one goose has to carry that extra burden alone. Did you also know that if one of the geese gets injured, the whole flock lands to attend to that goose before continuing the migration? You'd never catch a Canadian goose saying "Why should MY son have to be slowed down because YOUR son is a problem in the flock?"

Just like geese in a flock, bees in hives, ants in colonies, cows in herds and people are social creatures. We are hard-wired as a species to live communally since our survival requires a collective living arrangement. Just as the geese need the flock for migration survival, we need our tribe if we are to reproduce, feed and raise our youngsters.

We hang out in groups as families, classrooms, teams or communities. Because there are grave consequences if we don't have the security of being in a group to ensure our care and survival, we humans can't rest until we feel we belong and are accepted by others in our group. We use the words *connection, bonding* and *attachment* to capture the phenomenon of needing to know that we are accepted and loved. It's "Job #1" for people.

When children feel they belong and are loved and accepted, you'll know this by their ability to reach out socially to others, to enjoy independent time and not demand you keep busy with them. They'll be co-operative as a result of feeling they are part of the group and they will want to participate in taking care of the group's health too.

I Need to Believe I Am Capable

Will your children develop abilities, or prove their bigness by bossing others?

The urge to grow, mature and develop is in each of us. Babies want to learn to crawl and to communicate. Toddlers and preschoolers want to play "grown up" with toy cell phones and plastic shaving sets from Disney. Teens want to wear makeup and drive. It's all about moving from immature to mature, from incapable to capable, from being dependent to gaining skills that allow for your autonomy and self-direction. We all need to have choices and options to exercise. Competence is what freedom is about. Without it, we are enslaved.

However, we are guilty as a society of infantilizing our children, keeping them in a dependent state as long as possible. The life expectancy for homo sapiens was at one time only about 20 years. Today's 20-year-olds are only just finishing school and starting life! I'll bet a 20-year-old caveman could cook something more than Ramen Noodles. Between moving out of our cave dwellings and settling into condos, the life of children has drastically changed.

Today's children are given little chance to develop their own abilities. There are a number of different reasons for this. We're busy and have no time for pokey learners, and we don't like the look of the crocked corners and wrinkles that come when we allow a four-year-old to make a bed. Also, we enjoy feeling important and needed, so we don't want to stop being the caregiver and instead stimulate our children's independence. Where would that leave us?

On a deeper level, a big part of the problem resides in the fact that adults simply hold a low estimation for children. We think they are far more incapable than they are, and we don't trust them in general. Blunt, but true.

Somehow we think that without us around our children would never eat right, never get any sleep, never hit the books, and most certainly they would never say please and thank-you without first getting a poke in the ribs.

We parents sure are a bunch of naysayers with our constant negative nagging: "You'll cut yourself, you'll fall, you'll get cold, you'll get hungry, you'll fail."

Children need to feel they are capable. This is empowering. It allows them to exercise self-direction and autonomy. It's what self-esteem is built on. If we interfere with the child's ability to develop or if we lag behind in handing over to them what they are capable of doing for themselves, we'll see them find alternate, negative ways of achieving a sense of their own power.

I Need to Believe I Count
Will your children participate or retaliate?

Children need to feel they are valued. That can be in the form of casting a vote, sharing an opinion or doing a deed. We all want to count for something. Otherwise, why were we born?

We seem to understand the importance of this crucial C for adults, but children need it too. It is through service and contribution that we all feel our lives are worth something. We need to feel we are part of something larger than ourselves; a cog that helps to make the whole mechanism work.

Children used to be relied on to contribute. Having a child used to mean more hands to work the land; they were seen as an important asset. Now economists predict having a child sets you back about $100k and you still aren't guaranteed they'll visit you in the nursing home; they may be too busy working on their careers after that university education you paid for. Modern society has generally stopped calling on kids to pitch in and share the family load.

We don't ask their opinions, we don't use their talents and we don't ask for their ideas. We don't give them a function in our families. No egg collecting, cow milking or manure shoveling for this generation. We don't even ask them to do the dishes anymore. They are expected to do nothing but play and study. I know that sounds like utopia to overworked parents, but people are designed to be in service of others. THAT is what makes us mentally adjusted. People caring for people. It's the "give" part of the "give and take" equation that makes our symbiotic relationship satisfying. We especially shortchange children in this department these days.

I Need to Believe I Am Courageous

Will your children try new and challenging things, or avoid them?

Put down the superhero cape; that is not the kind of courage I am talking about. There are no dragons to slay today. The courage I am referring to is the profound kind. It's having the belief in ourselves that we can face challenges and stumble through life's roadblocks in a rather imperfect way, making mistakes, revealing our inadequacies and imperfections to the world. It's about being okay with "looking bad" because other things are more important. Can you make a mistake gracefully? See it as a learning experience? Do you avoid things that you think you'll fail at, only showing your good side? Children with this crucial C are confident and they will try new things. They have a resiliency to bounce back.

When we have the crucial C of courage, we stop being interested only in things that feed our ego and so we are free of the fear of "failing." We don't concern ourselves with impressing people, with others' judgment, with "winning people over" or "pleasing."

Once we feel courageous we accept that we are all humble humans, no better or worse than another. We stop trying to prove and protect our worth, and instead we are ready and able to accept ourselves, flawed as we are, and ready to live in the service of life. Period. Now tell me that doesn't sound like Nirvana. It does sound a little Buddhist in tone, doesn't it? Courageous enough to just BE without need of grasping, attachment and anything else you can remember from your yoga class. It's all pointing to the same human experience of needing to accept and be at peace with ourselves, right now, as we are in this moment.

For children this is especially critical, because adults seem so consumed with having children "reach their potential" that they send an ongoing message that as of right now, they are not good enough. If they bring home a test that they got 98 percent on, we ask how they lost the last two points. You're always two points from being okay in someone's eyes if you play that game. The courageous child doesn't.

Just to recap. Our children need the 4 Crucial C's. If they can't get these C's on the positive side of life, in ways that are appropriate and co-operative, they'll attempt to get their needs met on the negative side of life. These are mistaken approaches, or misbehaviors that are non-helpful and disruptive.

• •

New Insight #4: Children need to find their 4 Crucial C's. They will try through positive means first, but if they must, they will turn to negative means.

• •

As parents in the middle of a discipline crisis, we will need to know which C is deficient. Which C is your child trying to obtain?

To decipher this, you will need to think of yourself as a diagnostician. Before prescribing nitroglycerin or a Tums, doctors need to know if the patient's chest pains are due to angina or indigestion. Likewise, a child seeking connection is not going to respond to being given more opportunities to be capable, just as surely as a deficiency in calcium can't be cured by taking vitamin E.

We need to view our children's behavior as symptoms that hold important information. They are a key to understanding our children and a way of accessing their private world. Don't be so quick to want to get rid of misbehavior at any cost; we have to study it first! It's important evidence at the "crime scene," and we don't want it to disappear just yet.

The next time Zack spazzes out because you refuse to turn the car around and go back to the drive-through window to ask for the *other* Happy Meal toy, you can now say to yourself "Hey—excellent. I am just reading this parenting book and look—what luck!—here is an example of some misbehavior now. I hope Zack keeps this up for a bit so I get lots of good data." Well, maybe at least it will make you smile for a moment and ease the tension.

Let's continue reshaping our attitudes about misbehavior and mistaken approaches by adding our next new big insight to the equation: our role in creating and sustaining misbehavior.

Care to Dance? It Takes Two to Tango

Can you tell the difference between a fox-trot and a waltz? The tango and the Charleston? No? Okay, how about the Macarena and soldier-boy? Ahhh, now *those* you know!

Each of these dances has its own unique style and movements. They are highly identifiable with people moving together in a synchronous, predictable and consistent fashion that makes these dances recognizable and repeatable. We see these very same qualities in the patterns of interactions that are the "kerfuffles" we have with our children; it's a predictable, repeatable pattern between two synchronous partners.

Let's face it, that blowup in the front hall about how the bus is coming in two minutes and they're going to be late, and how you will not drive them if they miss the bus . . . if I were a fly on the wall in your foyer, I'd be having a déjà vu nearly every day! It's always the same thing, morning after livid morning.

New Insight #5: Misbehavior is a co-created experience.

In family systems counseling, we don't just look at the dawdling child and his or her bad attitude in the morning. The situation is not conceptualized as a bad child who needs to smarten up. Nor do we look at the adult and blame solely his or her parenting approaches.

What is identified as being problematic is the pattern of interactions between parent and child. They co-create a pattern that is recognizable, that is consistent, that plays out regularly and in which each partner knows every dance step.

In family systems theory, the interactional patterns or "the dance" two people create together are the focus of our intervention. Neither the child nor the adult is "the problem."

When things go squirrelly and your children start to misbehave, try thinking about their actions as being a subtle way of asking you to dance. They know how to act in ways that will engage you. They commence their behaviors with the implicit desire to evoke a certain response from you. They expect your response. They *want* your response. While this is all pre-conscious, it is still a calculated maneuver. When they zig, you zag. When they throw sand, you come running.

It may seem a bit odd to think that our children act in ways that would make us run to scold them. But it all serves a purpose to them, and that purpose is part of what we must come to understand. When we agree to "dance," we interact with our child in ways that meet one of their needs and fulfills one of the missing Crucial C's. Here they are:

When I don't feel connected—I will seek undue attention.
When I don't feel capable—I will seek power over others.
When I don't feel I count—I will seek revenge.
When I don't feel courageous—I will seek to avoid.

Attention, Power, Revenge and Learned Helplessness are the four mistaken goals that discouraged children seek when they don't have the 4 Crucial C's fulfilled positively.

Next, you will learn how to recognize which dance you are participating in, so that you can learn to apply effective new parenting tools for each situation.

CHAPTER THREE

NITROGLYCERIN OR TUMS?

In the last chapter, I shared a new perspective for thinking about children, their motivations and behaviors. We learned about people's need for the 4 Crucial C's and our children's quest to find them. I also shared the surprising news that we actually participate in misbehavior by agreeing to "dance" with our children in dysfunctional but utterly predictable and repetitious ways. Somehow these dances provide our children with one of the Crucial C's they're lacking, as we'll see.

This chapter is the last step to fully understanding the dynamic that has dogged you till this point. We are going to learn to become good diagnosticians so you'll know what exactly is transpiring when you're in the middle of those sweaty changing room antics we heard about earlier. You'll be able to say "BINGO, I got it! I know what is happening here. I see the dynamic!"

Once you get to that great epiphany, you'll be ready to charge ahead with the correct tools and tactics needed on a case-by-case basis. All the subsequent chapters will be dedicated to bringing you those tools. They are chock full of the democratic, non-punitive, non-reward-based tactics and techniques that I know you've been wanting to get your hands on. But first, let's learn to recognize those dances so we know if we need to be reaching for the metaphorical Tums or a nitroglycerin tablet. Remember my pledge to you: no more putting bandages on symptoms for your family. We're getting to the root of the problem.

FOUR DANCES AND THREE QUESTIONS EVERY BUDDING SHERLOCK CAN SOLVE

• •

"Holmes, you see everything."
"I see no more than you, but I have trained myself to notice what I see."
—"The Adventure of the Blanched Soldier"

• •

Put on your Sherlock Holmes hat, grab your calabash pipe; we're getting into some deductive reasoning. Learning to diagnose a child's misbehavior is like *Sudoko* for psychology buffs.

We have to learn to observe situations so we can properly identify the four dysfunctional dances that we do with our children. The process involves asking three questions every time you observe misbehavior.

Maybe you are thinking to yourself, "I am not a mind reader; how can I possibly know for certain what is going on inside my kid's head?" Have no fear—the three questions are actually about *you* and *your* observations of your children. You are already an authority on this.

So, Sherlock, What Do You See? What Are We Looking For?

Part of learning to recognize these "dances" is to watch for the interactions between ourselves and our children. Notice how little we learn about a dynamic from the typical parental description of a problem: "My child won't go to bed without crying and making a fuss. How do I make him stop?"

I know *nothing* from this small amount of information. Maybe he is getting poked by a spring in his mattress! To learn more about what is happening from a psychodynamic perspective, we need to think of the bedtime behavior as a small play with a cast of characters. These characters have dialogue and stage movement and they deliver their lines with emotion.

I should be able to visualize the action in my head by knowing who said what to whom, how the other person reacted and all the backing and forthing between the characters. And I also need to pay attention to how the scene ends. What was the big finale? After all, *something* had to happen to make the episode come to a conclusion. That's key information too.

With that in mind, let's hear the bedtime story again, this time with the scene set and actors in position. Compare this to the original telling of the tuck-in:

Everything was going well, but as soon as I finished tuck-ins and said "Good night, Ethan," he started to cry. I went back to his bed and I kissed him, reassured him that he was okay and told him to go to sleep. I felt guilty because I had worked late again and I hadn't had time to play before bed. I left him crying and joined my wife and his older sister in the living room. I no sooner got seated when he called out for a drink of water. I can't say no to a kid who needs water, so I got him a glass and sat on the edge of his bed while he drank it. I made some joke like "Whoa, you camel. You must have been thirsty!" and we both had a laugh.

I settled him back in bed and headed downstairs again. A few minutes later, Ethan cried "I have to go pee." I knew he just had all that water and he's just started potty training, so I wanted to encourage him. I went back upstairs and put him up on the toilet, then grabbed a book from the book bin so I could read a story to him while we waited for him to pee. After about five minutes I started feeling frustrated. Finally, I said, "Forget it; let's go back to bed." I hoisted him up to the sink to wash his hands and then took him back to his room, where I tucked him in again. Finally, I joined the others.

A few minutes later, Ethan called out "Daddy—I left Fluffy downstairs." I was aggravated by this because he can't sleep without Fluffy, so I had to traverse the stairs once again, bringing Fluffy to Ethan. When I got there he said "PleeEEASE—Just lie with me until I fall asleep." I was annoyed by how the tuck-in was going, but I knew if I stayed, he'd be asleep in a minute. By that point I was irritated by all of the going up and down the stairs. So I did lie beside him, and sure enough he was asleep in a few moments.

Okay, so now we have an interaction to study! We already know a lot about this scenario from the general principles we've learned: We know that all (mis)behavior serves a purpose, so this is not just some random happenstance. It's a child's creative endeavor to accomplish something. Now we are trying to tickle our brain to figure out what exactly the child gains or achieves from his choice of behavior (the repeated calling out for Daddy to help him with water, peeing and fetching Fluffy, then, ultimately, lying with him while he falls asleep). We know it must be something worthwhile since he repeats the strategy every night. We also know that all benefits to be gained come from the *other* actor on stage with the child, in this case Daddy, and that benefits are social or relational in quality. What could that possibly be? Well, we only have to narrow it down to one of four possibilities since young children only have four goals they pursue. Dad's responses to Ethan serve as one of:

Attention (a mistaken approach to achieving the crucial C of connection)

Power (a mistaken approach to fulfilling the crucial C of feeling capable)

Revenge (a mistaken approach to finding the crucial C of feeling as if he counts)

Avoidance (via assumed inadequacy, learned helplessness. This is a form of protection used when we feel we don't have the crucial C of courage.)

If you guessed that Ethan's goal is Attention, you are right. Parents often diagnose misbehavior as a result of the mistaken goal of attention. We hear parents say "He's just doing that to get my attention," but how do they know that for sure? I want you to have the definitive answer, not just a guess. Let's get the proof and ensure total confidence in your diagnoses.

To do that, we need to ask Dad the three diagnosing questions:

1. What do you do?
2. How do you feel?
3. How does your child respond?

Each of the four dances has characteristic answers that will allow you to make a proper diagnosis. To ensure accuracy, you *must* answer all three questions.

Now we will get a bit more complicated—let's look at each of the four goals one by one, and find out the answers to each of those identifying questions. I will provide you with a table summary at the end of the chapter that you should bookmark and keep as a handy reference guide while you are practicing the skill of making diagnoses in the weeks ahead.

With time, the need to refer to the table will disappear, and you'll be able to immediately diagnose the goal without any formal process, just as a bird-watcher improves her ability to "spot birds" and identify them without having to pull out the *Peterson's Field Guide to Birds of North America.*

You'll come to know these dances very well. The better you are at spotting and properly identifying misbehavior, the faster you can grab the appropriate tool and nip problems in the bud. With time, misbehaviors of all kinds can disappear all together—forever.

Understanding the Attention Dance

We agreed that Ethan was seeking the goal of attention. Look at how creative Ethan had to be! He has already discovered from past tuck-ins that crying and asking for things like water and to pee has a 100 percent success rate, since Dad can't seem to ignore these seemingly valid requests. Ethan might have already tried other ways, such as asking for another story. But, if Dad said "No, no more stories," and always refused that request, then Ethan learned that asking for more stories is not effective, and he moved on to others tactics.

Children experiment with behaviors and keep the ones that elicit the response they are seeking. Ethan's behavior allows him to stay in the spotlight. He manages to engage his father in some form of socializing for an additional half-hour after his bedtime. Dad has

"Ethan matters" to deal with and so he is tied up and can't engage with Ethan's mom and sister.

What would happen if Ethan gave up these behaviors? If he didn't cry and make requests, Dad would finish tuck-ins in a few minutes and then socialize with his sister and mom instead, and Ethan would be ignored.

Children who have the mistaken belief, "I must have attention in order to know that I belong and am important," will seek out any behavior that gets their parents to stop what they're doing and pay attention to them. Some kids will do this by being silly; they will jump around in some crazy dance that becomes their signature piece. Some children decide to take on a persona, as in "I am not Marcie. I am a cat . . . meow!" and suddenly you have a "cat" at the dinner table who would like her dinner served in a saucer. Perhaps your kids have discovered that they can enlist your attention through helping them, so they feign helpless in order to have you "care" for them by brushing their teeth, zipping their jacket, tying their shoes, putting on their coats or cutting their French toast for them. Other children will want you to feel worried, so they will bang their heads, or make themselves fearful. If people worry about you, that proves you're important to them. Attention-seeking kids will also discover ways to be a general nuisance and pest. They might whine, spill or blow bubbles in their milk. They might discover that making weird throat noises and clicks and clacks gets people's attention. They might complain of feeling sick in nonspecific ways, or be dramatic when they get a small scratch. They may try to impress you with feats at the park, showing off to you while yelling "Watch this! Watch this—NO HANDS!" Perhaps they talk too quietly, or too quickly, yammering on in a non-stop streak so fast you can hardly catch what they are saying. Perhaps they have learned that if they struggle and fidget they can get the teacher or Mom to sit with them and discuss each homework question one on one. The possibilities seem endless, don't they? It can be relatively easy for children to get what they want through these behaviors: they can be very effective. Take note: if you combine a couple of these tactics you can easily end up having a child mistakenly labeled ADD or ADHD.

These are just some examples of the myriad behaviors a child might stumble upon. The list is long, varied and diverse. However, seeing something you recognize in this list of behaviors doesn't necessarily mean that your child's goal is attention. We must pay attention to the response and reaction the behavior elicits. We have to ask all three of the questions in order to make the right diagnosis.

Question #1: What Do You Do?

What is your reaction to your child's pestering and clowning and repeated requests for water after tuck-ins? When the dance is attention, our response is to give attention and typically it comes in one of two forms:

1. Verbal attention in the form of nagging, reminding and reprimanding

    or

2. Non-verbal attention in the form of service. (You find yourself doing things for your child that you know full well she could and should be doing for herself.)

When you are watching the scene play out, check and see if you are saying any of the following lines:

"Stop that."

"Let's go."

"That's enough."

"What did I tell you?"

"Don't do that."

"I told you once already."

"Put that down."

"Don't hit her."

"Gentle hands, please."

"Get up."

"Get off."

"Eat, eat, eat!"

"Where is your scarf? Where is your bag?"

"Did you brush, did you flush, did you say thank you?"

"Don't pick it, kick it, wipe it, touch it or throw it!"

Notice these are all lines you have said a hundred times before, and probably you say them again and again in about three-minute intervals. Your kids *know* they should get off the couch when their shoes are on. They don't lack knowledge about how to use the couch properly. They know shoes should be off, just as sure as they know that keeping them on will bring about your usual spiel.

So, NO they are not deaf or a glutton for punishment. They are successfully engaging your attention—in a negative way. Bad press is better than no press at all, right? Better to act in ways that stimulate a lecture from Mom than to be ignored by her.

This is why most parents have difficulty with their children interrupting them when they talk on the phone. As soon as you pick up the phone it announces to your children, "You are about to be ignored; I am now giving my attention to someone else." Now the child who was playing happily on his own is suddenly yanking on your pant leg like a monk tolling a bell, incessantly chanting "Mom, Mom, Mom, Mom, Mom. . . ." And what do we do? Cover the mouthpiece and give them attention in the form of a verbal response "Shhhh—please, don't interrupt I am on the phone." (As if they hadn't noticed and as if they didn't know not to interrupt—dah!)

Not all attention has to be verbal, though. You don't *have* to talk while you do up a coat, but still the attention is on your munchkin and her coat, and *not* on the computer or *not* on her little sister who is getting ready to go out too. You can't dress someone without attending. Your focus is on your child—even if the words are not coming out of your mouth. So if you find yourself doing things for your children that you know full well they could be doing for themselves, you are probably in an attention dance.

I say "probably" because we can't decide definitively until we answer *all three* questions.

Question #2: How Do You Feel?

The attention dance can make us feel irritated, annoyed, frustrated or worried. These are the low-grade emotions that tell us that we're bothered by having to engage with these distractions. We find our child's antics taxing and tiring, sort of irksome. We don't want to have to deal with them. We'd rather these behaviors weren't happening, so we feel a bit put off.

And now the last question:

Question #3: How Does Your Child Respond to You?

What is their reaction to your nagging and "doing for" them? If your child's goal is attention, then she will be responsive and stop. She will quit bubbling the milk, go back to bed after peeing, get off the couch when you point it out to her—yet again. Your child has received your attention, so your actions are effective—BUT—only in the short term. With attention as the child's goal, we see the characteristic resuming of misbehavior almost immediately. Children either start up again with bubbling their milk, or they switch it up and move onto another trick they have up their sleeve that is equally frustrating to you. Now, instead of bubbling milk, they bang the table leg with their foot.

The overall feeling is similar to swatting at a fly that keeps buzzing around you. *This* is the attention dance:

1. You remind, nag and do for your child.
2. You feel annoyed and irritated.
3. Your child's misbehavior stops temporarily, only to resume again with the same or a different but equally annoying misbehavior.

Understanding the Power Dance

Let me describe another scene with different actors playing out a dance on a different stage:

> *Maddie calls her dad at work from her friend's house.*
> *She wants permission to stay at her friend's house after*
> *school. Dad says no, he wants her to go home to do her*
> *schoolwork. Maddie gets upset that her dad won't give her*
> *permission and she argues with him, saying that he is being*
> *unfair and unreasonable. She doesn't understand why she*
> *can't stay. Dad tells her that she has to go home to do her*
> *schoolwork before she plays with her friends. He argues*
> *that she is the one being unreasonable. After all, she just*
> *spent all day with her friend at school. She won't let up on*
> *her dad, saying, "It's only two math questions—it will take*
> *15 minutes, big whoop." Dad is getting cross. He yells, "I*
> *don't want to talk about this anymore. Just go home; I'll*
> *see you at supper." Maddie slams down the phone before*
> *he finishes talking and stays at her friend's house against*
> *Dad's wishes.*

Hmm . . . I don't think we are in Kansas anymore, Toto. This is definitely NOT the attention dance anymore, is it? This has a whole difference nuance. Can you tell from this description that the actions, reactions and emotions are all different? More intense? If attention is like swatting a buzzing fly, then power is more like being in a tug-of-war.

Children with the goal of power have two basic styles or approaches: either they are the kid pulling on your rope, or they act as the "anchor," the guy whose job it is to stay firm and show you that you can't pull them. They just stay put. One is aggressive power, and it's usually recognized by parents since it is so in your face. But resistive or passive power is often not detected as easily. Here is a quick chart to compare the two:

Style of Power	Aggressive Power	Resistive Power
Role of Child	Rebel / Oppressor	Resister / Stubborn
Typical Behaviors	Argues Blows up / explosive Short Fuse Tantrums Refuses to follow rules Lies Defiance Directly contradicts	Lazy Sloppy Late Endless excuses Agrees, but doesn't do Moves slowly
Belief Behind the Behavior	"I only count when I can show you I am the boss."	"My power and significance lies in not letting anyone boss me around."

Source: Adapted from the work of Dr. Richard Royal Kopp

You will find that in a family with siblings, one will have the style of the rebel and the other sibling will want to find their own unique niche or role in the family, so they opt for playing the resister. Sadly, the rebel tends to get punished far more severely in our society of "bully-phobic" adults. This can lead to a perceived favoritism, which deeply discourages a child and fuels more misbehaviors. With either kind of power dance, the same three questions apply. Let's have a look:

Question #1: What Do You Do?

With power, we aren't lecturing and nagging our children with simple comments to correct their behavior as we did with the attention-seeking child. Instead, things have taken on a heated intensity. It's a fight we are in, so we do all those fighting things: yelling, screaming, arguing, being physical and punitive. Do I need to say more? You know when you are fighting with your children.

Question #2: How Do You Feel?

There are several emotions to look for: If you feel threatened, challenged or defeated it's probably a power struggle. However, the biggest emotion to watch for is anger. Sure, your stubborn re-sister may make you feel irritated at first, but this type of behavior will also escalate—for you! Little Johnny may still be parked in front of the fridge door, refusing to move until he gets his fruit roll-up, but your emotions at his relentless, solemn search for more power are going to move from irritation to anger pretty quickly.

This is such an easy way to catch yourself getting into the power dance. There is a noticeable shift when we go from being irritated with our children and their shenanigans, to getting fed up and mad. This is a red flag that we need to watch for. Anger tells us that we have entered the power dance, either directly, or as an escalation from the attention dance.

Question #3: How Does Your Child Respond?

Here is another differentiating characteristic between the goal of attention and power. With attention, the child stops what he is doing and then resumes; stops and resumes, but always at a constant level of annoyance.

With power, however, we see behaviors escalate. Mom yelling at Jennifer to get off the couch doesn't work. Jennifer doesn't stop. In fact, not only does she not stop, she tries to "top her" somehow; maybe by yelling louder, or saying harsher words, or possibly by hitting or kicking, knocking things over—you know the drill. Of course, Mom's behavior escalates in kind. After all, she just tipped over a houseplant and there is potting soil all over the rug now! With Maddie, we saw the escalation from a request and a denial to Dad getting terse and then angry, and the trump card: Maddie hanging up on him. It is a progression of bad to worse as the one-upmanship plays out.

Can you see the difference between attention and power as a diagnosis? Is the picture getting clearer? Excellent! Of course there will be times when in one "scene" the goal shifts or it takes a bit more of your Sherlock abilities to tease out a clear diagnosis.

Let's test you: Do you remember Karen and her monkey-man who is running around the change room instead of getting dressed? She starts by feeling irritated. He is clowning around. She does a lot of reminding. Do you think it is the attention dance? Hmmmm. If you don't follow the protocol of working through the three questions, it's easy to think that. But let's double-check:

Karen starts by nagging and that is all we hear of her behavior really, except that it ends with her "snapping." Snapping means she has been getting more and more angry without expressing it, until she finally explodes. That means she may be under-reporting her emotions or is less emotionally honest with herself than she could be.

When she does nag, her child doesn't stop and repeat, as is the way in attention-seeking. His clowning sounds like something a person does if they want to be the centre of attention, but he is really being a stubborn resister. He is refusing to get dressed, and in a sense taunts her with behavior that really says "Na-na—you can't make me."

She also asks me, "How can I just *make* him listen?" Anytime I hear a parent use that line "make them" I am suspicious of power issues.

It may be that it started as an attention dance and morphed into a power struggle as Mom got fed up. When she has finally had it, she gets angry and more controlling, and unwittingly kicks off a power struggle. Her inability to get him dressed and out of the change room as needed seals the deal for me. I know it's power because Mom is *powerless*! That is why she calls me for help—to get some power over the situation that is defeating her.

You've got a huge foot up now on understanding and making sense of the crazy-making behaviors that probably have prompted you to read this book. I have two more dances to run through with you before we close the chapter, but you are getting so good at this process now that these last two will be a breeze.

Understanding the Revenge Dance

If children continually try and fail at finding their significance and sense of belonging in the family through power tactics, over time the retaliations grow more and more intense and severe. When parents constantly work to win power over children and keep them subdued, the relationships suffer. The continual fighting and punishments lead children to eventually come to the conclusion that they are, in fact, unlikable. They will conclude that they have no power in the family, and that they are "bad." Further abhorrent behaviors convince others to think the same. Children may shift tactics to try to prove they are "someone" by hurting others as they perceive they have been hurt. This kind of acting out is an attempt to say, "Hey, I won't let you hurt me like that. I am someone! I need to feel like I count for something, and you can't discount me this way."

Of key importance for parents to understand is that revenge is retaliatory. A child *never* seeks revenge first. Revenge is by its nature "getting back at someone." It occurs when we are hurting our children and they are letting us know. Sadly, we are often so busy punishing them for their actions that we miss our part in the creation of the problem, and we don't catch the hidden message they are trying to send us.

> *Mom arrived home to discover Oliver and his younger brother in the basement. They were creating a concoction with some fluids from Dad's workbench. Mom was furious! She stormed at Oliver, "What are you doing! That is dangerous. What are you teaching your brother? You could have blown up the house. Do you want to die?" The boys knew they were into mischief, but when Oliver tried to explain that his younger brother had heard at school how to make a bomb and they were just trying to see . . .*
>
> *Mom didn't want to hear anything about it. "I don't care! Oliver, go to your room right this instant. I've heard enough. I don't think a boy who is acting like a five-year-old should have a 10th birthday party. I am canceling the cake we ordered and telling your friends the party is off."*
>
> *With that, Oliver went to his room and his brother went upstairs to watch TV. Mom was still fuming while she cleaned up. Later that night, when Mom was in Oliver's room, she found he had drawn a small picture on the wall of what*

looked like a witch. Under it, he had written "Mom." She was
appalled that he had defaced the wall, and hurt by what he
had drawn.

You can bet that Oliver is in for more punishment and hurting now that his wall drawing has been discovered. He wanted his mom to discover it. He wanted to hurt Mom as he feels she hurt him. He acts instead of speaking. He doesn't say, "I am hurt that you only reprimand me while my brother gets off scot-free." He doesn't say "I understand that what I did was wrong, but canceling my birthday seems like too big a punishment for the crime. I was not trying to hurt you with my experiment—but you are intentionally hurting me by canceling my party and calling me a child. I am tired of always being responsible for my brother and how things will impact him, as if you care more about him than me."

I wish children could speak these words, but instead they act out. We need to be able to learn these diagnostic skills to deduce what is happening for children since they cannot simply tell us. In the chapter on dealing with revenge, you'll learn how to get this important information from you child. Every person has his or her own subjective reality. It is their truth, and for children who have the goal of revenge, we need to understand that though we may not have intended to hurt them, they are feeling hurt—and they are striking back.

Here are the three questions to diagnose revenge:

What Do You Do?
Punishing, retaliating, wanting to play the victim . . .
When people are hurt, they have an assortment of responses. Sometimes they play up feeling hurt in an attempt to make the other

person feel guilty. I see parents fake crying, even saying, "Mommy doesn't like it when you hit her. Look, you made Mommy cry." The motivation for doing this is punitive; it is a form of punishment. You can't cover up your motives by saying you are trying to teach empathy—bah, humbug—the intention here is to make the child feel bad!

We also have this "Oh yeah, mister?" self-talk, that says, "I am NOT letting him get away with this!" and so we feel justified in taking the child out at the knees. In this way of thinking, children are seen as some evil force and we are like Batman over Gotham City, justifying our violence in the name of restoring order. Suddenly, retaliation and punishment take on a golden sheen. For example, when Nolan spits on you for saying, "We have to go home now," you feel downright righteous saying "That's it—home, and straight to bed."

How Do You Feel?

Appalled, shocked, hurt, spiteful . . .

It's a good indicator that you are dealing with a revenge dance when you have your wind knocked out of you just thinking about what your child has done to you. Here is this child you raised robbing your wallet and hawking your mother's wedding ring. There is a feeling of disbelief that floods your system: you can't believe this is your child. You discover your child has actually had a BM in your closet, not on the floor, but with terrific aim—in your purse—and you know it was not a mistake but directed at you personally! How broken do our hearts feel when we finally say to ourselves, "I am not sure I even love my child anymore"? This deep response alerts us that we are in a revenge dance with our children; we feel shocked and we even feel like striking back.

How Does Your Child Respond?

Vindictive, abusive, devious, stealing, self-destructive . . .

Oh yeah, with the revenge dance, you are *so* getting it back. After all, your children are out to hurt you and they know your vulnerabilities. I trust them to succeed.

They'll stare you blank in the face and say, "I wish you were dead." Or, with seething bitterness they say fatal words like, "I wish I lived with my father; he understands me!" and "I wish you weren't my mother—you're a whore." Of course there is also running away from home, living in the streets, drug use (NOW she'll pay for this), and more. But the younger set usually sticks to "pooh-pooh head" and "You're not coming to my birthday." So, count your lucky stars we're on the case early.

Just as attention rolled into power, now we see power rolling into revenge. The deeper the discouragement, the further we go into the four goals of misbehavior until we finally arrive at the fourth and final goal: assumed inadequacy or learned helplessness/hopelessness. We end at the avoidance dance.

Understanding the Avoidance Dance

Oh, how did we ever get here with our children? Thankfully, our children are so wonderfully resilient that we rarely do reach this level of discouragement, but we still need to be able to detect it should it happen.

Children who attempt to get you to participate in the avoidance dance have lost any hope that they can find their significance and belonging in either the positive or the negative side of life. They have tried all the tactics they can think of to show some strength, some way of being successful at something, but every effort has been met with failure and defeat. They are bankrupt of ways to prove their worth. Children who continue to feel that they fail us, let us down, disappoint, come up short and have no talents or attributes of value, eventually feel worthless. They have one last tactic: give up and stop trying. It's really rather brilliant on their part. After all, you can't fail if you don't try, right? Avoiding is useful for them: they make themselves helpless and exaggerate it in such a convincing way that others come to believe them. They are excused from participating and so avoid tasks which will reveal to the world their worthlessness. They save face by doing nothing at all. There's no embarrassment, if you don't try. Hell, you're not even in the game! We pity them, we worry about them, and we give them alibis to opt out, believing they can't manage.

Of course, all of our "help" in lowering the bar for them, actually reinforces their belief. "If Mom doesn't think I can do it, I guess I can't." Eventually, parents throw up their hands and say, "I give up. I can't do anything with this kid." So we stop putting demands on them: BINGO—the strategy works.

> Jenny's parents were called in for another parent-teacher meeting to discuss her progress at school. She was struggling in every subject and had significant problems with reading. The teacher was concerned because Jenny already had extra help in class, plus some tutoring through the school's reading recovery program, yet still there was no improvement. Nothing was working. During the interview the teacher asked what Jenny did at home. Mom shrugged her shoulders and said, "Nothing anymore. She doesn't want to help, and when she does it's usually so poorly done that I have to do everything again myself. It's not worth asking anymore."

Jenny has figured out her own way out of her perceived rut, but it's costing her soul. She is severely discouraged about herself and her worth. She is avoiding life instead of meeting life's challenges, and she will not be able to integrate herself into the larger social world if we don't intervene. She is using the veil of being helpless and hopeless to reduce the demands on her and to keep her safe in a small private corner of the world, unable to grow or develop.

Here are the three questions to diagnose the Avoidance Dance:

What Do You Do?

Oh! To be the ambitious parent of an unambitious child. We work tirelessly to find out "what the heck is wrong with this dud of a kid." Or we're certain there is some disadvantage at play, so we try to help.

> "I think I need to get him tested. Maybe he has autism or Asperger's or something. He's just not your average kid, is he?"

> "I think I'll make another appointment with Miss Johnson to see how he is doing this week. I am not sure anything we've tried is getting through to him. He certainly is not going to be able to do a speaking presentation."

> "I am looking into home schooling. She doesn't like the loud classroom, and all the other children intimidate her."

Parents are critical and judgmental. In their quest to find out what is wrong with this kid, they constantly compare their child to others. "Why can't they do what all the others are doing?" Parents pressure their children in subtle ways by being hyper-vigilant about how their children are doing. Parents tend to over-help, excuse or rescue the child. They also give up on the child, thinking that any efforts they have made so far all seem useless, so why bother? Their efforts seem like an act of futility that never pays off. "Why should we try so hard if our kid won't even make the slightest effort? Doesn't she see that everything we are doing is to HELP her? Why doesn't she grab the lifeline we throw? If she doesn't care, then there is nothing more we can do either...."

How Do You Feel?

It's common for feelings of futility and apathy to set in. That's all part of the dance. Don't underestimate the child who has mastered avoidance. They are working to make all your parental efforts fall short, so, of course, you're going to feel discouraged. At some point we all feel like throwing in the towel. Don't feel rotten about that. Instead, marvel at how brilliant your children were at getting you to back down and avoid your own discouragement. Powerful thought, isn't it?

How Does Your Child Respond?

Here we are busting a gut to reach these children and they give us nothing in return. It's as if they see us coming and retreat further. They are remarkable at holding their position or stance on NOT getting better, at NOT showing improvement. They really are like the living catatonic, unfettered in their commitment to stasis and inertia. And they do it so well. We don't feel duped or like we need to make them snap out of it; we really do believe in their charade. We become convinced that they really are incapable at a root level. It doesn't seem like a façade to us. We're their parents, after all. We'd know it if they were faking it—wouldn't we?

So now you have had a tour through the four goals of misbehavior and how to diagnose each one. I have emphasized the goal-directed nature of the behavior and how our interactions provide the outcomes our children are after. Keep in mind that while I have presented these as four "distinct" dances, they do run into one another. I mean, you can hardly have a fight with someone without paying attention to them, right? And you are going to feel hurt if you had a fight and got wounded, so the line between power and revenge can blur as well. The tools you will acquire as you read on will help you to move between the dances and use appropriate parenting techniques, so don't worry about a bit of overlap in the particular dynamics you are experiencing.

As children get older, their needs and motivations become more complicated. Children under the age of ten will always be striving to attain one of the four goals we have studied here. In children over ten, you will find that while these goals may still apply, there are a few more that come into play that are beyond the scope of this book—things such as "thrill-seeking," "masculine/feminine identification," and so on. However, these initial four dances are by far the most common, and the most powerful for you to understand. As promised, at the end of this chapter is your handy-dandy reference chart.

A word of caution about your new understanding of your child's inner motivation: these powerful forces are not understood consciously by our children, and they shouldn't be revealed to them unless with the guidance of a trained professional.

Pulling your child aside and saying, "Hey, Sue, I'm reading this book and the author says you're a tyrant who wants to take over the king's chair I've abandoned. Apparently, it's all about power for you. Also, you're just doing this because you don't really believe you're capable or competent, so you are trying to compensate for what you think are shortcomings," is not only bad form—it's dangerous! Please, never use this information as a weapon.

Take heart in knowing that with this new information you will be able to do your part in changing your actions. However, also know that the ultimate decision to change always lies with our children. We can proceed in ways that either improve or erode our family dynamics. We can create an environment that challenges children to alter their mistaken beliefs and their approaches to life. But we also have to respect the democratic idea that children are responsible for their own choices and decisions. It may also be that for some children the training and expertise of a therapist or counselor is required. That's okay, too. Just be aware of it, and don't read into it something more dramatic than it is.

Before you put the bookmark in and turn off the bedside light, I have one tactic to kick off your morning that you can try right away. It's a tactic that *every* parent can do immediately, in every situation. I call it, "Doing the George Castanza." Remember that episode of *Seinfeld* when George has the realization that everything he does has a 100 percent failure rate? He has an epiphany and decides that instead of doing his usual thing, he'll try doing the opposite. In psychological circles, this is called the "fallacy of first impulse," and it speaks to the idea that our knee-jerk reactions, our first gut impulse, is the payoff our children are hoping for. If you want to start making changes right away, disrupt your repetitive dance by NOT doing whatever it is you have been doing, over and over and over again. Hey, if George Castanza can do this, there is hope for all of us!

Four Goals of Misbehavior

THE CHILD'S GOAL	PARENT FEELS …	PARENT REACTS …	CHILD'S RESPONSE	CHILD'S BELIEF	HIDDEN MESSAGE
Undue attention (to keep others busy or to get special service)	· Annoyed · Irritated · Worried · Guilty	· Reminding · Coaxing · Doing things for the child he/she could do for him/herself	· Stops temporarily, but later resumes same or another disturbing behavior	I count (belong) only when I'm noticed or getting special service. I am important only when I'm keeping you busy with me.	Notice me, involve me. I want to connect.
Misguided power (to be the boss)	· Provoked · Challenged · Threatened · Defeated	· Fighting · Giving in · Thinking "You can't get away with it." · "I'll make you." · Wanting to be right	· Intensifies behavior · Defiant compliance · Feels powerful when parent is upset · Passive power	I belong only when I'm boss, in control or proving no one can boss me. "You can't make me."	Let me help. Give me choices. I want to feel capable.

(continued)

(continued)

THE CHILD'S GOAL	PARENT FEELS …	PARENT REACTS …	CHILD'S RESPONSE	CHILD'S BELIEF	HIDDEN MESSAGE
Revenge (to get even)	• Hurt • Disappointed • Disbelieving • Disgusted	• Retaliating • Getting even • Thinking: "How could you do this to me?"	• Retaliates • Intensifies • Escalates the same behavior or chooses another weapon	I hurt others as I feel hurt. I can't be liked or loved.	Help me, I am hurting. Acknowledge my feelings. I want to feel I count.
Assumed Inadequacy/ Avoidance (to give up and be left alone)	• Despair • Hopeless • Helpless • Inadequate	• Giving up • Doing for • Over-helping	• Retreats further • Passive • No improvement, no response	I can't belong because I'm imperfect, so I will convince others not to expect anything of me. I am helpless and unable. It is no use trying because I won't do it right.	Show me small steps. Celebrate my successes. I need to know I am okay as I am, and help building up my courage.

Adapted from *Positive Discipline for Preschoolers*. Jane Nelsen, N.Y., Ballantine Books, 1996.

CHAPTER FOUR

THE ATTENTION DANCE

It wouldn't be suppertime at Josie's house without the five-year-old twins chasing each other around the kitchen island where she is trying to pull together a meal. They race like madmen running with the bulls in Pamploma. Sock-footed and sliding, they bank the corners, smashing into cupboards as they go. It's fun! And especially since Mom shrieks (which sends them giggling) and engages in her nightly repertoire of "Boys, stop that. Boys, I mean it. Someone is going to get hurt! Boys, that's enough. I'm working with a hot skillet; be careful."

Ahhh, good times. I don't think there is a parent among us who hasn't had some firsthand experience dealing with an attention-seeking child.

With Susan, it's her little guy. Seems he likes to get chased when it's time to get his PJs on each night. "Stand still; come on. Let's go; help Mommy."

Gerald refuses to take his kids with him on trips to the Home Depot anymore since he spends all his time policing, telling his boys, "Don't touch that. Put that down. Don't run in the aisle—watch where you're going—you just about hit that cart!" Since when does buying a sheet of drywall take three hours and two Tylenols?

But, isn't it a relief to know that our kids are not just being inconsiderate pests or whining nuisances? Now that we are sympathetic (because we understand the goals of misbehavior and we have done our diagnosing), we can see that it's a child's gallant efforts at connecting with us. Understanding the human dynamics helps us to have more empathy for their behavior.

That said, having empathy doesn't mean we have to accept it or excuse it. No—that would be permissive parenting. Understanding the dynamic helps us to see with a fresh lens, so we are less discouraged ourselves and better able to handle the situation effectively. Ultimately, it's the key to plotting our course of corrective action.

With the child whose goal is undue attention, we need to address the mistaken belief "I only count when I am being paid attention to." We know that our children are important and significant *all* the time, and not just when we are attending to them. However, our typical responses to attention-seeking (nagging, reminding or giving of service) don't counteract this internal belief. In fact, our responses encourage our kids to keep seeking connection through these negative means. So our knee-jerk reaction can't continue—we have to do the ole "George Kastanza" by NOT giving our prototypical responses in these situations. Instead we have to show that co-operative, non-disturbing behaviors yield our engagement.

Let's look at how, in the moment, we are going to step out of this attention dance:

1. Do not give undue attention when your child is demanding it from you.
2. Give your child attention in the form of real connection.
3. Avoid the traps that parents typically fall into: stonewalling, random reinforcement and others.

The parenting tools you will learn are:

1. The delicate art of ignoring
2. All action, no talk
3. Distraction
4. Redirection
5. Natural consequences
6. Logical consequences
7. Training for independence

And, the tools for the longer-term solution:

1. Be present and leave space for independent entertainment.
2. Catch 'em being good.
3. Build the relationship connection in the deep and rich way the child seeks.

Are you ready? Let's start loading up your democratic parenting toolbox. I am going to go over each of these and show you examples of how they look in various situations of attention-seeking. You can begin implementing these immediately. I will give you lots of tools specific to attention-seeking and then you can choose which one seems best for the encounters you're facing. If you understand the principles behind the misbehaviors and why the tools are effective, you'll be able to switch your tactics as needed.

THE DELICATE ART OF IGNORING

If you have properly diagnosed the goal as attention, and if the situation allows it, simply say nothing and pay no mind. Your child will quickly realize her behavior is no longer successful in engaging you. Once the behavior loses its effectiveness, the child will stop. A 14-month-old with a shrill shriek usually succeeds in getting everyone in the room to look her way, cover their ears and say something along the lines of, "whoa—that hurts our ears. Please use your *inside* voice." Instead, I recommend you ignore the shriek by not flinching, not looking her way and not commenting at all. Simply go about your business as if you didn't hear it. After a few days your child will not waste her time with it. It's not effective, so why bother?

I have had a lot of firsthand experience of the effectiveness of this approach as a nursery school teacher, and I've seen undeniable evidence of this with the children of deaf parents. Their parents don't respond to screaming, so those kids come up with different schemes for grabbing attention, such as vibrating and shaking.

I worked with a family whose child found every opportunity to eat paper. Mom had to follow him around the house to keep him "paper proofed." If she turned her back for a moment, he would be hiding somewhere eating a tissue or toilet paper. We diagnosed this as attention-seeking behavior and talked about Mom being non-responsive. Of course, she was worried about the possible health concerns, but her doctor assured her that a few days of paper in his digestive system would not be harmful, so she agreed to ignore the misbehavior. Two years of paper eating ended after three days when Mom stopped attending to it.

So, first see if you can simply ignore the misbehavior. I understand that this will feel permissive to you at first, but if you're accurate with your diagnoses, and you experiment with this tactic, you'll gain confidence in its effectiveness. Give it a try.

Common Parenting Pitfall: Stonewalling

Who knew there is a right and a wrong way to ignore? When I observe parents implementing my advice of "Ignore the undue attention-seeking behavior," I see them instead ignoring the child. They may turn on their heels and walk away coldly, as if to say, "You are a pest and a nuisance and I am not going to let you bother me. I am going to make you pay for your misbehavior by ignoring you." This kind of response is punitive in nature, because it is intended to hurt the child. To be more dramatic about it, it's like saying, "You misbehaved and upset me, so now you are dead to me." Ignoring the child means we have put up a wall and disconnected from them emotionally.

Given that these children are missing the crucial C of connection, and attempting to solve that by seeking undue attention, our stonewalling and disconnecting just makes matters worse.

This really speaks to the parenting dictum of separating the deed from the doer. It's only the behavior that is not worth our responding to. We *do* want to notice the child and become involved with him positively. If he picks his nose in front of you, it is an invitation to the dance. Decline! Decline by not offering a payoff: ignore the behavior, and instead find positive ways to engage your child.

ALL ACTION, NO TALK

Of course, we have a hard time ignoring behavior that is destructive or unsafe. In the democratic model, we are charged with maintaining individual rights *as well as* the social order, so sometimes we must take action.

In those situations, I recommend "zip the lip" and just "do" whatever corrective action is required. For example:

> If a child is jumping on the couch, instead of saying, "Get down from there!" simply walk over to the couch and assist her down with no words.
>
> If a child is hammering on the coffee table, take the hammer away.
>
> If he is picking the leaves off a plant, move the plant up out of reach.
>
> If a child is pumping the foaming soap 15 times, remove the soap dispenser.
>
> If she is hanging precariously off the railing from the tenth step, put her on the ground.

Each of these actions will maintain the order of the house without saying a word. Attention-seeking children will not be upset, as they already have a good idea they should not be doing these things. They will know their tactic is not working anymore.

DISTRACTION

Let's not lose sight of the fact that our ficus-leaf-plucking-child is seeking connection! It's only because he can't seem to accomplish connection positively that he will turn into Edward Scissorhands. Recognize in the moment that your child's actions are calling out for a positive connection with you, and give it to him by distracting from the misbehavior to something positive.

"Hey, Edward, do you want to help me water the plants? I have a special watering can with a really cool spout you might like learning how to use. I can show you!"

Because Edward's intention was to engage with Mom, the offer to learn about the water solves his need to connect with her. This is all the child guidance required in the moment. Let's look at another example:

> Jenna takes her son Ben to the grocery store. He is bored watching Mom shop. He starts pulling reams of plastic bags off the roll in the produce aisle. Mom correctly diagnoses this as a bid for her attention and finds another way to engage his attention. "Ben, can you help me pick five apples?" While Ben starts picking apples, Mom quietly re-rolls the bags he pulled out, but no words are said about "the bag incident."

Her son already knows not to unroll the bags—that was the point of his actions. He doesn't need a lesson in "shopping behaviors"; he needs an experience of positive connection. Mom's distraction is the corrective measure, and that is sufficient. Anything more is overkill. Save your energy.

> Josh keeps kicking the back of Mom's car seat as they drive to school. Mom bites her tongue and instead of saying for the umpteenth time how she is bugged by his kicking, she turns her attention to Josh positively and distracts him from his kicking by asking if he wants to play the alphabet game. Josh says, "YES! And there is 'A' in Acura on that car beside us!" The kicking stops and the game begins.

Let's pause for a moment. Are you thinking, "Good lord! Must I always be the one to engage him? Can't the little bugger just let me drive in peace? I don't want to play the alphabet game every day.

Sometimes I want to just listen to the radio. And I can't always drag out the shopping by waiting for my child to pick apples. Can't they just be patient for a change?"

My answer is, Yes! You are so right. A truly co-operative child will see that some situations in life require patience and coping with boredom. However, in order for children to be willing to be co-operative in these situations, they must have all their Crucial C's met. We are on the right path with these techniques, and in time, your children *will* develop patience. Hang in there while we nurse them back to being fully C-positive. It takes time, but you will get there.

REDIRECTION

Distraction and redirection are similar, but slightly different concepts. Distraction is meant to hijack the child's attention from what he is doing and then focus it on something completely different ("Oh, Yoo-hoo. Look over here!") Redirection, on the other hand, involves showing the child the proper way in which he can carry on with what he was doing.

> Jordan is playing with the garden hose in the backyard. He turns the hose onto the lawn furniture and Mom lights into him: "No, bad boy, I told you before, not the furniture. We sit on those! Don't spray there; you're making a total mess of everything. How many times do I have to tell you that people are going to get wet pants if you spray the chairs? Don't do that again. Do you hear me?"

Compare that verbose excitement to a redirection response:

"Can you come with your hose and water my vegetable garden, Jordan?"

Jordan still gets to use the hose, but he is redirected to an activity that is useful and positive.

Now here are two questions for you:

1. If you were Jordan, and you wanted Mom's attention, which of the above responses would encourage you to water the furniture again? The longer, more dramatic response, right?

2. If you're a child who is struggling to overcome feelings of not belonging or of not being significant, which response is likely to help you overcome those discouraged feelings about yourself and your place in the family?

NATURAL CONSEQUENCES

Natural consequences are a wonderful, impartial way for our children to learn about their behavioral choices. Let me explain what a natural consequence is, how children learn from them and how to use that wisdom in your parenting.

To understand what a natural consequence is, let's break down the term. In this context, "natural" refers to the laws that govern the natural world. It covers such things as gravity, thermodynamics, friction and inertia. "Consequences" refer to demonstrable outcomes.

If we want children to learn the natural laws that bind us on earth, then they need to experience how different actions result in different outcomes. It helps children put together cause-and-effect relationships. They love learning that a large rock dropped in a mud puddle makes a bigger splash than a little rock, that if you let go of the string of your helium balloon it will float up and up and up, and that if you don't blow on your hot chocolate, you can burn your tongue on the first sip. They don't need to know that $E = mc^2$

in order to operate according to that truth; they simply need to experience cause-and-effect relationships.

The reason children learn so quickly with natural consequences is because the outcomes are 100 percent consistent. Gravity's laws are always in effect, so every time you let go, your toy falls to the ground. The laws of thermodynamics always yield a burn if you put bare fingers on the glass of the oven door when the cookies are baking.

Natural consequences can teach our children, if we would just step back:

> If you don't eat—you get hungry.
>
> If you don't wear a coat—you get chilly.
>
> If you don't wear socks—you get a blister.
>
> If you don't keep your fingers out of the way—you get a pinchy on the cupboard door.
>
> If you pour the milk too fast—it drowns your cereal.
>
> If you don't rinse the soap off your hands well enough—they feel sticky.
>
> If you build your blocks too high—they fall over.
>
> If you leave your snack unattended—the dog will eat it.

We tend to spend our parenting energies warning our children about the consequences, hoping that our nagging and reminding will help them avoid experiencing any nasty consequences. The trouble with our strategy is that it is actually the *experiencing* of a consequence that does the teaching. Getting a blister is what teaches you to wear socks, not Mom's lecture. In fact, Mom is interfering with little Tina's learning if she chases her around the room in order to get those socks on her.

Now that Mom has stepped in, Tina will not learn the sock-blister connection. Instead, she will learn a nifty way to engage Mom:

Don't put on your socks and then Mom goes, blah-blah-blah, chase, chase, chase, and then she dresses you! It's awesome.

Instead, Mom can share her concerns and leave Tina to decide: "Sometimes when we don't wear socks we can get a blister that hurts, but I trust you to decide for yourself about your socks." Done. *Finito.* You've put it out there for her, and she can weigh that information, which may may or may not sway her decision.

> *Donna sits on the side of the sandbox to keep an eye on Owen while he plays because he keeps trying to put the sand in his mouth. "Yucky," Mommy says each time. "Not in the mouth, Owen. Yucky—sand is for the sandbox. Put it down. Not for eating," and so on.*

Owen is learning that every time he lifts his sand-filled fist to his mouth, his mother starts talking like a windup doll. Instead of learning not to eat sand, he is learning how to make Mommy talk! Mom could instead say nothing, let Owen experience a mouthful of sand, and he would quickly realize that it is indeed "yucky."

So when possible, why not take a load off and let Mother Nature do her thing? We work hard enough as parents. Let's enjoy being effective while doing nothing for a change. Of course, there are a few situations when using natural consequences is not advisable:

1. **When the consequence is too severe.**
   A little burn from touching the uninsulated side of the toaster is one thing, but I am not advising you to let your children play in traffic (I think that legally covers my butt, right?). Obviously, we must keep our children safe. However, I am suggesting you take them out of the bubble-wrap packing, and stop interfering with their learning. "Teachable moments"

will actually protect them in the long run, as they will learn a healthy respect for life and its risks and dangers.

2. **When the consequence is too far in the future.**
Natural consequences also won't work on youngsters if the time between the cause and effect are too far apart. Cavities take years to set in, so I would not use natural consequences to deal with your toothbrush-avoidant tots. They have to be able to connect the dots in their heads between cause and effect. Don't worry, when natural consequences aren't the right tool, you've got plenty more to reach for—read on!

3. **When too many others are impacted.**
If the tobogganing party is today, I would not use natural consequences to teach about the benefits of dry, warm legs. If one child is freezing, everyone's fun comes to an end. In this case, let the child know that snow pants are a requirement of attendance. She can leave them in the car and put them on if she gets cold later, but she has to have snow pants with her. No snow pants is not an option today.

LOGICAL CONSEQUENCES

If our children learn so quickly from natural consequences, why not use similar methods to teach them about the social laws that govern people in a democracy? We can't all run around doing as we please. Chaos would reign! We need our children to learn the social conventions of our society. They need to learn that freedom comes with responsibilities:

> The freedom to eat sugary foods comes with the responsibility to take sugar off the teeth.

Those unwilling to take responsibility for removing sugar from their teeth, lose the freedom of eating sugar.

or

The freedom to ride a bike comes with the responsibility to wear a helmet.

Those who do not wear a helmet lose bike privileges.

After all, if our children can learn the cause-and-effect relationship "If I let go of the spoon—the spoon drops to the floor," they are also capable of understanding the relationship between freedoms and responsibilities.

Logical consequences teach exactly that relationship. They are amazingly effective, *if* we create them correctly and apply them properly. But boy, oh boy, is there room for a lot of mistake-making with this tool! Let's make sure you get it all straight in your head so you can start using this technique.

To ensure that a logical consequence isn't punitive, the consequence must meet two criteria: It must be *related* to the behavior (hence the name "logical") and it must be *revealed* to the child in advance.

Related Consequences

Your child needs to be able to see the cause-and-effect relationship as being logically connected. For example, children can understand that since meals are eaten at the table, if they get down from the table, their meal is finished. That seems logical. But, let's look at a common mistake with this technique. Compare these two approaches:

Approach #1: "If you get down from the table, you'll lose your Nintendo DX for the night."

Approach #2: "If you'd like to eat dinner with us, you need to stay at the table. If you choose to get down from the table, that's okay too, but you will lose your Nintendo DX game for the night."

Hmmm. Which version is better? The first example is clearly a punitive threat, while the second one seems better on first reading. After all, version two is stated very nicely, and the child is given options. But read them both again. They are really both punitive. In each case, the parent wants the child to stay at the table, and she is letting him know she will punish him if he doesn't make the choice she would like him to make.

In both examples, the parent's motivation isn't to teach, or to maintain order in the family, but to "stick it to him" by doing something that will sting a little. These are just tidied-up versions of power wielding, and both are manipulative. We're trying to dress up that bovine in a party frock again.

Likewise, it's punitive to deny a cookie at the bakery because your little Mario Andretti drove his trainer grocery cart into that lady with the high-heeled shoes. A more logical consequence (one that your child will understand as logical) is that the cart is taken away if he can't accept the responsibility of pushing it carefully. Freedoms and responsibilities go together. Cause and effect: if you don't accept responsibility, you lose your freedoms.

Revealed in Advance

In a democracy, people are free to make choices, but every choice has an outcome or consequence. Our children are free to choose their behaviors. However, in order to make an informed decision, they need to know what options they have, and they need to understand the consequences of each option. "If I choose A, B will happen; If I choose C, D will happen. What will I decide?"

In action, it looks like this: "If you would like to walk, you have to stay beside Mommy. If you run ahead, you'll have to go in the stroller."

Walk—stay out of the stroller
Run—go back in the stroller

This way, your children can make their choice with full knowledge of what lies ahead.

Parenting Alert

Now let me just give you a quick heads-up on something to expect that might snag you. Chances are you will be faced with a child who says, "I'll walk, I'll walk," but while saying one thing, she's doing another. She says she chooses to walk, but in reality she starts to run! This sort of thing happens all the time. The mouth and the feet are in disagreement.

When this happens, it's the *action* that indicates your child's decision, not the words. When she takes off, you pop her in the stroller and say, "I see you have chosen the stroller." Yes, she'll probably cry and protest that she "said" she would walk. That's okay. You can be empathetic. "I am sorry you're disappointed with your choice; you can decide differently next time." However, when a child makes a decision, please let the decision stand.

Does this sound like something you're ready to try? Let's look at some more examples to make sure you've got it.

Social Law: We draw with our crayons on paper only.
Logical Consequence: If you choose to draw on the table, walls or something other than paper, the crayons will have to go away. You can try again in the afternoon.

Social Law: We don't bang our cups on the table; we keep them still.

Logical Consequence: If you choose to bang your cup on the table, it will have to be removed. You can try again at the next meal.

Social Law: We need to feel safe in our home.

Logical Consequence (if child is hitting or kicking): If you can calm yourself, you can stay here with us; if not, you need to be alone. If child keeps hitting: I see you need to go, come back when you are ready to play safely. (Note: this is essentially a non-punitive form of a time-out. I never use the word "time-out" when talking to children.)

If your child won't stay in this "time-out," or if he comes right back and hits again, you have a power struggle on your hands and attention tools will no longer work. More on "power tools" (I just had to say that once in this book!) in the next chapter.

Common Parenting Pitfall: Stating the Consequence *After* the Action

There are two major pitfalls with Logical Consequences that trip up nearly everyone. The first is to state the consequence without warning, *after* the action has taken place:

- "That's it, mister; it's back in the stroller for you!"
- "I've had it! I'm taking away that cart since you can't push it safely."
- "No more crayons for you; you're writing all over everything."

Yes, these are logical, but the child was not given the information ahead of time, while she was in the process of deciding whether she would walk or run, push the cart safely or whack it into people. The child with the crayons might have decided to keep the drawing limited to the paper if he knew that by choosing to write on the table he would lose his opportunity to color for the rest of the morning.

Common Parenting Pitfall: Failing to Follow Through

I can hear your exasperated protests: "But I *did* tell him not to run. But I *did* tell her not to crayon. I've been telling them that a thousand times! They won't listen. That is why I am reading this book!"

Nagging your kids and reminding them provides undue attention. Instead, you need to follow through with the consequence. This is what is tripping you up. Our children learn from what we do, not from what we say. If we reveal the consequence in advance and then don't follow through, we are teaching our children that we don't really mean what we say. They become "mother deaf." Worse, when we do finally muster the will to follow through, they perceive the consequence as erratic punishment. The child thinks, "Hey, yesterday you said if I ran with my cart you'd take it away, but you didn't. Why should I think you would today? That's unfair!"

In order to make logical consequences effective, we have to replicate the properties that make natural consequences work so brilliantly by being both consistent and non-judgmental.

Be Consistent

If children are jumping on the couch, the "natural law" of gravity teaches that they could fall off and bump their heads. True, but let's be real. It's not their heads we are worried about: it's ruining the upholstery on the new couch. (Sorry kids, your heads are tough; fabric isn't.) No natural law of fabric deterioration is going to help us teach children about why they shouldn't jump on it.

So how can we best teach the "Leon's Law" of no-jumping-with-grimy-street-shoes-that-will-take-years-off-the-springs-and-ensure-the-couch-is-ruined-long-before-you-make-the-last-of-the-ho-ho-ho hold-the-payments?

If we nag and remind, we risk teaching our children how to engage our attention negatively. Instead we can create a logical consequence.

To be effective, we need the cause-and-effect relationships to be related as well as revealed in advance, and we have to follow through 100 percent of the time, consistently and without judgment, just as it is in a natural consequence.

If we want our children to learn that couches are not for jumping on, then every time they jump on the couch, we must remove them. Not just when we feel energetic enough to get up, go over there and put them down on the floor. Did you catch that? EVERY TIME. After all, gravity doesn't sometimes take a holiday and leave that dropped spoon suspended in the air. How confusing would that be?

We have to actively follow through with carrying out the consequence each and every time. Yes, it takes energy, and we can get all bummed about that (oh no, more parenting work to do!) but I promise you this: a child who experiences a well-constructed and consistently implemented logical consequence will learn quickly.

If you only nag and remind about consequences, the behavior will continue on and on and on. Your nagging will continue on and on and on. Comparatively speaking then, over time, you'll spend *less* energy dealing with misbehavior if you're effective at implementing logical consequences. Trust me, ineffective nagging goes on *forever*.

Common Parenting Pitfall: Random Reinforcement
When we stop doing the attention dance with our children, there are a few stages we tend to go through:

1. Initially, when we stop giving undue attention, children will usually re-double their efforts. The behaviors get worse as they work harder to get us back into that attention dance that used to work so well for them.

2. If they consistently experience a lack of the payoff they used to get—even when they try harder—the behavior will begin to taper off.

3. Finally, they will abandon the behavior all together, satisfied that it's no longer useful, no matter how persistent they are or how hard they try. That is the day we are looking forward to!

However, if at anytime, in a moment of weakness you do provide the payoff, the children learn to hang in there, keep at it, be persistent, and occasionally they'll get that response that they are seeking. If you've been ignoring your child's repeated, attention-seeking calls for "Fluffy, a drink of water, and 'I gotta pee,'" on most nights, but every now and then caving in—uh-oh. You can bet your child is now going to keep calling and trying for MUCH longer, hoping that tonight is another one of those nights where you have a lapse.

This occasional payoff is called "random reinforcement." It is the strongest enforcer of human behavior there is! Just take a stroll through any casino and you'll know how powerful it is. All those mesmerized people, pulling on slot machines, gambling away the family's grocery money and their old age security checks are entirely unable to leave. They have the same internal dialogue as your child: "This time I'll be lucky, just one more time. Maybe this is the one. I do hit the jackpot occasionally, so I just have to try again."

If you stop dancing in your old ways, and you no longer provide that payoff response, be adamant with yourself that you'll hold firm to your strategy until your children reach the conclusion that their behavior is no longer effective.

Be Non-Judgmental

Have you ever noticed how Mother Nature doesn't lecture or moralize? When our children make their behavioral choices, we simply have to follow through with the consequence. We don't need to be dramatic over the choices they make.

If they color on the table and you have to take away the crayons, do it in a firm and friendly manner. No need to add, "I guess we won't be able to make his birthday card now. Poor Daddy, he'll be so sad."

If they get up from the table and we follow through with the consequence of taking their plate away, we don't need to make a big display of scraping their meal down the incinerator in a huff. "Well, that was a big waste of food! Don't come to me if you're hungry later."

If they throw a toy and we follow through with the consequence of removing the toy, we don't need to add, "I guess you can kiss your Buzz Light Year goodbye, eh?"

Bite your tongue and don't indulge yourself in the cathartic "look at what you've made happen now" or "I told you so" moment of parental superiority. All those lines are punitive, and while we may think we are driving the point home, we are instead hindering the powerful learning of the logical consequence itself. Now it's between you and your children, instead of between their choices and the outcome they experience. Get out of the picture! Move to the background, and let your kids learn from what happens.

• •

Say what you mean, mean what you say and follow through in a friendly manner.

• •

TRAINING FOR INDEPENDENCE

Never do for children what they can do for themselves. Attention-seeking children often discover the effectiveness of enlisting your service. It makes sense. What parent wouldn't carry an adorable child pleading "uppy?" or give a quick zip to a zipper she is struggling with? "Mooooooooommy, I can't do it. You do it." If we've been carrying them and zipping them into their jackets for years, why not one more time? These acts of "helping" only stimulate more moaning and pleading. Our children know that sometimes we'll carry them up the stairs, so why not try again? To eliminate this attention-seeking behavior, we need to put effort into teaching our children the skills needed for autonomy (how to put on shoes, cut their pancakes, zip a zipper and so on) and once they have learned, we must step back. It should be a moment of celebration. They have learned something new. WOW! At that point you can say, "Now you know how to do that all by yourself. You don't need my help with it anymore. Congrats! From now on, that is your job."

That is a very clear boundary or limit being established. To enforce the boundary we need to be consistent in NOT stepping in and doing our children's jobs for them. If they whine for you to cut their pancakes after they have learned how to do it, you can say, "That's your job. You're so capable!" If you're consistent with NEVER doing this job again, your children will cease trying to enlist your service in this area. However, you must not miss the clue that they are asking for you to be involved with them. So, move the conversation forward, off the undue attention-seeking and onto something else. "Which Teletubby is the purple one? And who exactly is that neurotic-looking fellow who lives in a pineapple under the sea?"

LONG-TERM SOLUTIONS

So, just to recap: your children want to feel connected, and they want to be noticed and involved. That's a really lovely thing if you think about it. They are working at being social. Fantastic! If they didn't strive for this, I'd be worried about them. Children are supposed to find connection, and their tenaciousness is wonderful—okay, frustrating, but wonderful.

When we face attention-seeking behavior we have to remind ourselves that our children are simply discouraged. Currently, they are not sure they do belong and so we need to help them. Here are three excellent ways for you to encourage your children to meet their crucial C of connectedness.

Be Attentive

Did I just write that for real? If ever there was a generation of "over-attentive" parents, it's us. We have such good intentions, but we make a mess of things when we try to be ever-attentive and fail.

Who can really stop life for 18 years and pay full attention to his or her child? In fact, that's sick advice. Do we really want to promote the idea that life shuts down and we all gather our chairs in a circle around Charlie who would like to impress us every time he burps or smiles? That is not having a relationship with your child; that's being an audience.

Strengthening connections to build meaningful relationships does require our time and attention, but not our eyeteeth and sanity too!

Don't Fake It

In our attempts to attend to our children like all the "good books" guilt us into doing, we end up faking our attention. Do we really have to watch and applaud *every* time they go down the big tube slide at McDonald's playland? Must we feel like an uncaring mother if we just take a five-minute hiatus and read the paper with our coffee? Heck, we already agreed to take them out for a "happy" flapjack meal so Dad could sleep in. Now we just want a few happy moments to ourselves. Is that too much to ask?

No. it's not. You can quote me. Far worse is to have our children shout "Watch me, Mommy; watch me, Mommy" and then to appease them with a robotic "Yeah, yeah, Mommy's watching" while we bloody well aren't—we're too busy finishing up the paragraph we're reading!

Don't misunderstand. I think you do deserve time to read the paper. I am suggesting you claim that time. The usual pattern is to feel guilty and to blow your kids off with half-hearted, partially frustrated attention (now THAT feels disrespectful and cold).

We've all been on the receiving end of that kind of attention. You know what it feels like when you're talking and your partner says, "Go on, I'm listening," but you see him checking work e-mails on his iPhone.

It is a far more efficient route to building good connections when we are fully present and fully in the moment. But that isn't the end of the story. We also need to learn to set clear boundaries around our time. It is perfectly acceptable, even desirable, to let our kids know when we need to put our attention elsewhere and to claim our rightful time to ourselves:

> "I want to hear everything you have to say, but I can't give
> you the time and attention you deserve right now because

I am in the middle of pulling dinner together. Can we find
time to talk after supper?"

or

"I would love to play dress-up with you, but not right now,
I am not in a creative mood. Can we make a date to do that
later? If I could just have a half-hour to get a few things
done, then I would be free and clear to have a game of cards
if you feel like it."

You'll find that your children don't demand your attention as
much if you stop faking or pretending to engage.

Encourage Independent Play

Instead of multitasking and having our heads in the clouds while
we are trying to connect with our children, make time to connect
with them and then step back and allow space for them to play
independently and entertain themselves.

Don't fret that this time is being wasted. Don't bother yourself
with eternally finding some "enrichment" activity. Believe me, it's
enriching to teach our children that we are not their entertainment
coordinator, and that they must learn to solve the problem of boredom. They will, if given the chance.

Make a part of every day "independent playtime," so children
have the expectation and develop the skills to make their own fun.
A great way to do this is simply to have nap time evolve into "quiet
time" as they get older and stop sleeping in the afternoon. Keep
the same schedule, but instead of sleeping, they can play quietly in
their room for a half-hour or 45 minutes. The whole house can be

quiet and calm, and everybody is expected to do their own quiet thing. Your batteries will be recharged and you too will be ready to be social and engage again.

Catch 'em Being Good

Our attention-seeking children have learned that they get more mileage out of us when they kerfuffle than when they "behave." We can switch that up by working harder to pay attention when they are indeed acting in ways we would like to see more of. Try saying some of these lines that you have probably thought, but maybe not shared with your child:

- "I enjoyed cooking dinner and overhearing you and your brother work so co-operatively on that puzzle."
- "What a joy it is to spend time with you at the table. I really like your company."
- "Thanks for letting me talk to the sales clerk about the dry-wall project I am working on. I appreciate your patience."
- "You are a great helper to me when we grocery shop; thanks for looking after the apple job for our family. You were very careful about choosing ones that were not bruised."
- "How nice to be able to watch you do up your own coat and look after yourself like that. You are learning so many new things!"

Make Deposits into the Emotional Bank Account

So, are you primed to start making essential deposits into the emotional bank account of your child? Children, like adults, need evidence of love. How do you feel close to your friends? Children? Spouse? Siblings? Co-workers? Have you thought about what that looks and feels like for you?

Therapists are taught to have "unconditional positive regard" for their clients. In attachment theory, they talk about achieving "emotional attunement" with your child, and, in Adlerian terms, we talk about being "encouraging." The key message here is to be in an active, caring, respectful relationship with someone who gets you, accepts you and revels in the marvel that is you.

In connected relationships, we feel supported and safe to be our authentic selves. We feel cared for, and we know that others genuinely wish for our happiness. How do we strengthen this bond with our kids? Here are some ideas to help get you going, but feel free to expand on the list:

- Spend time together.
- Anticipate and respond to your children's emotional needs.
- Treat them with respect.
- Listen more (a lot more) and talk less (a lot less).
- Let them take the lead in play.
- Be curious about their life: ask questions that show you are interested in them.
- Know the names of their teachers, friends and other important details of their lives.
- Share a hobby or project.
- Have them help plan something for the whole family (an outing, an activity, a games night, a special meal).
- Create family rituals—a pot of tea and beading, Tuesday evening board games, bike rides, an annual camping trip, Saturday free-skates at the arena, a hike in the woods to find things to decorate the Thanksgiving table with. . . .
- Show signs of affection.
- Write them a love note and leave it on a pillow or in a lunch pail.

- Take a day off work and pull them out of school to go on an adventure.
- Remember important happenings in their life and follow up: "How was choir practice?"
- Be attentive when they greet you.
- Ask them to explain things to you.
- Find out what their interests are.
- Read a book out loud to one another.
- Let them tell you about problems without interrupting to "fix them."
- Invite them to talk about their feelings, good and bad.
- Create common experiences.
- Invite them into the conversation.
- Ask their opinions.
- Sing together.
- Don't allow the phone to interrupt your conversations.
- Tell them about the day they were born, or what they were like as babies.
- Laugh together and share an inside joke.
- Pay attention to the little moments. These are more important than trying to build a relationship during the three weeks of holiday you get from work. Phone calls, text messages, love notes, checking in, a rendezvous for lunch if you always work late . . .
- Share a chore—shoveling the drive, raking leaves, cleaning the garage, washing the car, washing dishes. Use this time to lighten up, chat and be silly.
- Make up nicknames for one another.

Connection with our children is an ongoing process. If we make the investment, we will reap the benefits. When we are connected with our children, we want each other's happiness and will go out of our way to help those we are in good relations with. Our children will co-operate willingly!

If we can pay twice as much attention to constructive behaviors we'd like to see more of, our children will experience the crucial C of being connected to their families, and they'll alter their belief that they must be in the limelight to prove their importance. With all those deposits into their emotional bank account, they'll come to believe they are loved and important—always.

Now that we understand the dynamics of the attention dance, let's move on to tackle the dance of power.

CHAPTER FIVE
PARENTING YOUR LITTLE HITLER

If you've been resorting to a "wack-a-mole" style of parenting, in an attempt to subdue your budding tyrant from annexing the family, then this chapter on power struggles has the solutions you've been looking for.

By now you've probably noticed that as parents we can't actually MAKE our children do anything. When we try, we're met with two responses: Our "little pleasers" obey us, inspired only by their desire to outdo their siblings and "look good" (more on siblings in the next chapter), while the "tyrants" resist or rebel. But don't fool yourself; neither response is co-operative.

Instead of falling back on methods of domination to force obedience, we have to set our sights on winning co-operation and influencing the child. We need to shift the locus of power from external, parental control to intrinsic motivation, the lovely authentic kind that comes from within children themselves. Since we can't "make them," we have to "make them wanna" instead.

We can stimulate our children's willingness to be co-operative by creating the right conditions:

- Creating mutually respectful relationships, first between the parents themselves (I heard that snicker), and then extended to the kids.
- Empowering our children. Helping them find their crucial C of feeling capable by moving them progressively from dependence toward autonomy, re-calibrating our expectations almost constantly to keep up with their ever-expanding abilities.
- Connecting our family unit and making it strong so that the child feels a part of the "team" and is motivated to want to help the team as a whole, rather than adopting an "every person for themselves" mindset.

It takes time for these conditions to be achieved systemically in the family. One evening of withholding your usual yelling does not suddenly make the relationship respectful. But if you implement what you're learning in this book, I promise that with repetition and steadfast commitment on your part—it will come! Don't give up too early. The end result is so wondrous and beneficial for both you and your child, I know you'll agree it was worth your time and effort.

If that sounds too "pie in the sky" theoretical and you're thinking, "This lady doesn't know my Jeremy. We've been fighting to get him to clean his room for years, and even with all of that work, it still rarely, if ever, gets done," then let me offer you this: instead of reading on with a skeptical mindset, let's fast-forward to give you a glimpse of what we are shooting for. Then, with the end in mind, we'll go more methodically and pragmatically together through the steps of shifting power downwards in the family while still maintaining order.

PIE IN THE SKY

In a democracy, we need to balance one individual's rights and freedoms against another person's rights, as well as upholding the rules that sustain order for all. With freedoms must come responsibility: they go hand in hand and are inseparable.

If we don't accept the responsibility attached to certain rights, we lose those freedoms. The goal in a democracy is not to control people, but to attain liberty and justice for all (not just some). We create rules of order to help us function harmoniously together, and people have the power to change the rules of order by which they are governed. Okay, maybe Thomas Jefferson wasn't the most interesting guy to chat with over a lager, but he was on to something!

So what does democracy look like? Well, for example, democracy in our society dictates that I have the right to play loud music as long as it doesn't interfere with my neighbors' rights for peace and quiet. After 11 p.m., the law says I need to turn down my music since that is when society, in general, sleeps for the night; the laws have been created by the people to reflect the needs of the majority of citizens. This is a reasonable limitation to personal rights that is set to help the greater good. Some people are shift workers, and it's inconvenient for them, but they understand and care for their neighbors. They understand the inherent needs of the situation, so they adhere to the law (mostly). The law doesn't scare them into compliance; the ironclad logic of social living makes sense to them. If they want to change a law, there are well-laid-out steps to follow to present their ideas to the proper level of government for consideration (this foreshadows Chapter 8 on family meetings).

The law acts as a way of enforcing a boundary only if there is a breach. If people blare their music late into the night thinking,

"Neighbors be damned," we can see that they don't feel a sense of community and belonging that would make them care about their neighbors' well-being. Improving neighborly relations will stimulate a willing compliance more successfully than calling in the law enforcement officers, which would only provoke more neighborly unrest.

This example is a larger scale version of what can play out in the microcosm of your family. I am appealing to you to think less militaristically in your parenting and forgo the role of "policing" when it's not needed. Instead, take matters into hand through building good relations and winning people over. We seem more willing and able to do this with adults, but because of our old biases against children, we are often less willing to take this approach with them. But these attitudes can be overcome. Now let's take a look at how democracy works at home:

DEMOCRACY AT HOME

Jeremy's bedroom is always in disarray. His mom, Wendy, harps on him to make his bed and to pick up his clothes and use the clothes hamper instead of the floor. Jeremy always says he'll get around to it, and, of course, never does. Mom ends up picking up so she can at least get her vacuuming done. So far Mom has made no headway in getting Jeremy to take responsibility for cleaning his room. All they do is fight about it.

Let's look at how the rules of democracy guide our course of action. We could say that in a democracy people have a right (and are happier citizens) when they can "own land." It's almost primal to want to place a stake in the ground and claim our own territory.

Jeremy (nine years old) is now old enough to stake out his personal space in the house. He should be allowed to put that stake in the ground and to build and maintain his "castle" in whatever order he wants. If he shares a room with a sibling, his own space may be limited to his half of the room or his bed and a shelf, but, nonetheless, that is his sacred space.

In this instance Mom has no right to interfere with his quiet enjoyment of his private room, so long as it doesn't impact on others. If mold starts growing on his gym socks and the spores are floating into other rooms, then Mom has a right to speak up. But, give me a break, rarely does any room become an actual health hazard. Would the city officials condemn it? Mostly we make up bogus stuff like that to manipulate the situation in our favor. Kids have a hair-trigger detector for this, so don't even go there. You'll lose their respect.

A parent can't *make* her children clean their rooms. That is the children's responsibility and if you try, they'll resist. However, you can let them know that it violates your rights and freedoms to have to pick up clothes off the floor to vacuum. So, to ensure *your* rights are not violated, you can inform your child that you'll vacuum rooms that are picked up. After all, garbage collectors don't knock on your door if you forgot to put your bins out; they drive on by, expecting you to do your part if you want this service. Similarly, Jeremy has choice. The right to choose for one's self is to be free of tyranny. If we want to empower children, they need to be free to make choices (and to be accountable) for themselves.

Jeremy is empowered to decide whether he would like his room vacuumed. If he is so inclined, he has the option to pick up his clothes. If he doesn't care about a vacuumed rug, if he prefers to leave his clothes on the floor and forgo the vacuuming, THAT IS OKAY!

Can you handle it? Can you stand that your child has different values than you?

Even among adults there is wide variability in tidiness in the home. However, a child with an utter pigsty of a room is usually not expressing a preference so much as making a statement. It's an act of resistance. The slightest evidence of tidiness begins to feel like submitting to Mom's will. "If I make my bed she'll have got her way over me, so I had better not." Mom's urging for cleanliness is exactly what is preventing it. Oh, the irony!

If Mom wants Jeremy to care for his room, she must first stop fighting with him about it. Only then can she begin the work of stimulating him to co-operate. She can improve the likelihood that he will develop a desire to want to keep a tidy room. If she allows a pride of room ownership to grow, maybe allowing him to decorate his room to make it his own, Jeremy will probably start to keep a tidier space because he sees it's his room and it's nicer that way. Intrinsic motivation! Boys will care for their rooms the way they care for their first car, but you have to appreciate that black paint and strobe lights may be their style.

With our children, nearly any behavior that is an extreme aberration from the way most people function is stirred up by power struggles. Believe it or not, in the absence of discouragement and without interpersonal power plays, most children actually do get on with life the way the rest of us do. It's the truth. Sure, there are individual differences in how each of us prefers to do things, but mostly we're social creatures and eager to adapt. Encouraged children will mimic our ways of living fairly closely.

The aim of this chapter is to help you create a more democratic family and to help the resistant child co-operate. The more democratic your family becomes and the more the power is moved down from the ruling autocrat and is shared among all family members, the more harmony you'll experience. Ta da! There is your prescription for the power diagnosis.

We have work to do. In this chapter we will tackle power struggles by:

- Learning to get out of existing power struggles with a four-step model I'll teach you
- Discovering the power of choice and problem-solving
- Finding ways to prevent power struggles via empowerment

And, of course, I'll point out those common parenting pitfalls that trip us up.

D.R.O.P. THE ROPE MODEL FOR GETTING OUT OF POWER STRUGGLES

Jeremy's mom won't see a change in his bedroom's cleanliness until she figures out how to get out of the power struggle she is having with him. Well, I have very implicit instructions:

First—DON'T WIN. Sorry. I know you didn't want to hear that. However, it's important that you stop winning, because while you may get that one piece of broccoli you're so adamant about down your four-year-old's gullet, it only serves to sustain power struggles in the family. When we win:

- We model domination to our child, and they imitate us.
- We are treating our children with disrespect. We put them in the position of being a constant "loser" in life.

- We teach "might is right."
- We knock our children down a peg and they have to get back up, usually by retaliation and questing for more power.

Second—DON'T LOSE. Show some respect for yourself too! Speaking of modeling, we have to demonstrate self-respecting behaviors to our children. How can they respect us if we don't respect ourselves? We train people how to treat us, and it's not okay to be abused by another.

This is especially important preparation for the teen years when our parenting role switches to "trusted advisor." As our children get older, *they* decide whom they will be influenced by. If we want them to continue to look to us, we need their respect if we hope to keep our place on their list of key influencers. When we lose:

- We lose our own self-respect.
- Our children lower their opinion of us.
- We prove again that "might is right."

For example, if after denying your kids candy three times, you finally can't tolerate their whining and say. "Okay, but just one," you can bet they'll adopt that tactic as a regular modus operandi to getting their way, and think you a rather pathetic authority figure. We can't have that.

The trick is to look for that elusive third option: Truce. You don't have to play the game to the bitter end. You can decide to stop the game all together by dropping your end of the proverbial rope. If you leave the playing field, the child is left without an opponent. It is possible to make a pact with yourself to refuse to fight with your children. Tell yourself you are going to get all

Ghandi-esque and take a pacifist approach in your efforts towards peace. If Ghandi could do it with a country, we can do it with a couple of kids.

Instead of a win-lose outcome, we are searching for a win-win or a best-for-both solution. Please realize that this is not the same as compromising or negotiating, which I see with alarming frequency in families these days. Negotiating is not co-operating. It comes from a competitive mindset that is concerned with making sure no one comes out ahead of the other. It often leaves both parties agreeing to something neither of them wants, but satisfied that at least the other person didn't get his or her way either. *Yuck*. Where is the loving feeling in that?

If we shift our mindset and attitude from relying on disciplinary action, which fires us up to be punitive, and instead move into a problem-solving mode *with* our children, we'll be in the right frame of mind for success.

Co-created problem-solving is possible (and gratifying!) when you start using the tools I'll teach you here. But we must start by dropping the rope to end the tug-of-war we're embroiled in. When parent and child both grip opposite ends of the rope, the tension sustains the fighting conditions. All concerned feel they must flex their power lest they be dragged to the opponent's side and deemed a loser. Only when the tug-of-war rope is dropped can both parties be free to move in a new direction.

The D.R.O.P. model (outlined in the box on the next page) shows us how to make this move. When the rope is dropped and the power struggle is over, we can move to joint problem-solving during a time of peace, not fighting. That's when we'll find the answers to the problems that have been creating conflict. The sooner we get to this step, the sooner you will find harmony.

The D.R.O.P. Model

D = Determine you are in a power struggle. We always start with diagnosising the child's mistaken goal.

R = Re-assess the situation objectively. What's really going on here? A course of action is determined by what the situation demands happen right now, rather than personal opinions of my way versus your way.

O = Offer an olive branch. In power struggles, parents act in ways that are perceived as threatening and that invite defensiveness. Instead, show through your words, actions and body language that you come in peace.

P = Plow on positively. Get yourself unstuck by concentrating on you. Clarify your responsibilities and get busy managing yourself (not your children). Clarify what your children's responsibilities are and allow them to learn to manage their own business. Let them learn by allowing them to exercise their own choices, while holding them accountable for the choices they do make.

Let's look more closely at each piece of the D.R.O.P. model so you can get this happening in your home.

D: Determine You Are in a Power Struggle

We have already looked at the diagnosing process in Chapter 3. If you'll recall, the cardinal emotion is anger. It makes sense. Anger is an emotion that fuels us up to prepare for battle. It happens when we perceive a threat; in this case, usually it's the feeling that we are losing control and that our children are gaining control over us. Oh, you don't like that sensation? Neither do they! Hence the fight.

As we prep for battle, our adrenalin starts to pump, our muscles get taut and we find ourselves physically on high alert. When you feel angry and find yourself entering fighting mode, say "WHOA NELLIE—this is a power struggle. Let me stop for a moment and re-assess."

R: Re-Assess the Situation

So there you are, caught, rope in hand, wondering what the hell is supposed to happen now? Don't win—don't lose—HELP!!!

The next step is to take a deep breath and re-assess the situation. Clearly, by your child's resistance and the presence of a power struggle, there is a tipping of the power distribution, and that means there has been a breach of respect of some kind.

I have a little checklist in my head I consult:

1. Are the child's rights and freedoms being respected?
2. Are the parent's rights and freedoms being respected?
3. Is there a respect for the order of the family?

It's a tricky game balancing these against each other, but if you are aware of these three pillars of democracy, you'll get the hang of it. We have lots of examples coming up that should help illustrate that balance.

During conflict, however, we are just not very good thinkers. It's as if we're wearing blinders and have a one-track mind. We're so bent on winning and getting our way. Of course, the same goes for our children. Both parties are feeling defensive and inflexible. It's a formula for gridlock.

To get out of this gridlock, we must stop the personal power contest and instead look to a higher authority to determine the course of action required in the moment. That "higher authority" used to be the King's way, but in a democracy we have no King. Instead we have to look for a more global assessment. I refer to this as the needs of the situation, or the N.O.T.S. of the situation. What does the situation demand must happen right now, rather than going with personal opinions of "my way" versus "your way?"

Here are some examples:

- We need to brush our teeth because the plaque will cause cavities. Not because "I say so."
- We need to stay in our seats in the restaurant so that the waitresses are free to move about the aisles without worrying about bumping into people.
- We need to leave muddy boots at the door so the floors stay clean.

These are situational demands. They speak to "common sense" rather than idiosyncratic preferences or the "private logic" of any one individual. Here is another example:

Young children need to go to bed at (say) 7 p.m. because they need that much sleep to grow, be healthy and cheerful the next day. What dictates bedtime? You, or the needs of the situation? Many toddlers have erratic schedules and are sometimes still up at 10 and 11 p.m. Often this is because they are the children of a single parent who enjoys the time together in the evening. However, the true needs of the situation dictate that the child should be in bed.

So, when we ask our children to go to bed because "it's time" (dictated by the needs of the situation, which are consistent) and not because on this particular night "I say so" we can sidestep power struggles. As your children get older, and their need for more self-determination grows, you will need to be responsive to that shift. We can allow our middle-school children to take on the responsibility of deciding on bedtime, so long as they also accept the concurrent responsibility of getting enough sleep to be healthy, energetic and pleasant the next day. If they can't manage that task responsibly (with some practice), they lose the freedom to decide for themselves. We can then together come up with a bedtime that's suitable and let them try again at setting their own bedtime in a few months.

Analyzing the needs of the situation helps us to be objective. Often our preferred way will be the same course of action that the situation demands. But not always! Does this parenting hiccup ever happen to you?

> *Virginia's daughter refuses to eat her salad at dinnertime. They fight every night. Mom agrees it's a power struggle but is fixated on the fact that she is the parent and it's her responsibility to make sure her daughter is healthy and eating well. She asks me, "How can I make her eat her salad? Sometimes she sits at the table for up to an hour before she'll take a bite."*

If we stop and re-assess the situation, it becomes clear that the problem lies in Mom forcing her own solution to the dilemma of eating well. Mom thinks eating a salad at every evening meal is the best way, the right way, the only way to healthy eating. Is that true? Instead, Mom could put the problem out there to be solved together: "We need to be healthy and that means eating nutritiously according to the food guide; how can we get there?" Now there is a huge amount of choice. If Mom removes her blinders and identifies the problem she is trying to solve, she and her daughter can work together towards the goal of healthy eating in a myriad of ways and over the course of many meals that week, not by Mom analyzing her daughter's every bite. If the daughter has some choices and input, she will be more likely to live within the order she helped establish. Bingo! Co-operation!

Let's look at another situation and apply the idea of re-assessing the N.O.T.S.

> *Callum (28 months) refuses to get his diaper changed. Mom hardly has the strength to tackle him, let alone the dexterity to hold him down and try to get a poopy diaper off his*

corkscrewing body and flaying legs. It's a fecal disaster. "How
can I get him to stay still and let me change him, Alyson?"

It's a power struggle alrighty, and Mom is worried that Callum
will get a rash if she doesn't change his diaper. Her solution to the
problem of an impending diaper rash is to get that diaper off ASAP.
However, the current situation is simply that he is *in* a dirty diaper;
there is no immediate health concern or crisis. Mom's insistence
invites his resistance, so the best bet to getting the diaper changed
is to not fight over it. However, we can't be permissive, so we have
to look to the pillars of democracy to guide us again:

- Respect for self?
- Respect for others?
- Respect for order?

And ask ourselves: What do the needs of the situation dictate?
Callum doesn't want his diaper changed, and in a democracy,
he has the right to be in a smelly diaper (since we've ruled out health
issues), but respect for order dictates that if his pants are seeping
or wet, he needs to stay on a tile floor and be off any hard-to-clean
fabrics or carpets. Mom also has a right not to smell his bowel movements, and she can disclose this to him respectfully. Now, he is free
to decide for himself how he would like things to go. "I see you don't
want your diaper changed; that's your choice. However, soiled diapers
need to stay out of the living room, since we don't want poop on
the carpets and sofa. That's not okay. Come get me when you'd like
it changed and I'll help you. I'll be over here since I find the smell
unpleasant and hard to be around."

Children don't "love" being in their poop. Sure, they may not
mind it as much as an adult, but children don't have some burning

preference for a dirty diaper over a clean one. That is an example of the extremist behavior that is set up by being embroiled in a power struggle. Callum is fighting over being told what to do. He feels getting his diaper changed is submitting to his mother's will. He refuses to be controlled in this way.

Is it too much responsibility for a two-year-old to decide when he wants to get changed? How do you know when he can manage something like that? Two years old sounds really young! It's the parents' job to manage diapers *until* the child starts resisting and fighting with you over it. This is the great thing about trying to figure out what is developmentally appropriate in these situations. If there is a power struggle, it confirms that the child is ready for more power and control in this area of his or her life. If your children are fighting to get power, they are ready. Hand it over!

In Callum's case, I predict that he will test Mom and stay in a dirty diaper for a time. When Callum sees that Mom is no longer engaging in a power play with him, and when he believes she is not trying to manipulate or control him, then he will come to see the merit of having a clean diaper. He will want to play with Mom and sit on her lap and go on the couch, and if it requires a clean bum, he'll ask to be changed (intrinsic motivation). Since Callum came up with the diaper change idea, he is more likely to be co-operative about it. The act of a diaper change is no longer perceived as losing or submitting to Mom.

Do you see how this is all coming together? Okay, let's move on to the next piece of the solution.

O: Offer the Olive Branch

The universal signal of peace is the offering of the olive branch. We need to show our children that we are not fighting. When parents say, "I am not willing to fight about this," usually means, "I win, so don't fight me." That is no longer going to work.

As parents, we often appear to our children as threatening, and that causes our children to get their hackles up. We signal to them that we are being dominating without always knowing we are doing so. Children are very perceptive about such matters. We say, "Put your coat on; it's time to go," and they interpret our "Put your coat on," to be a command. They react to being "told what to do" while we felt we were merely stating a fact. It's like living with a hair-trigger. Boom—we're met with resistance. Their resistance says, "Don't tell me what to do."

If we follow the idea that for every action there is an equal and opposing reaction, we can choose behaviors that either intensify or de-intensify any given moment. If we get tense, they get tense. If we get calm, they get calm. Now that's powerful information we can use to improve matters.

Let me show you how to improve the way you communicate with your children so that hair-trigger doesn't go off on you. It's estimated that only 7 percent of communication comes from verbal content and a whopping 93 percent comes from body language. Let's look at improving both.

Body Language

Have you ever seen a grizzly bear defending its berries? They use their body language to communicate their power and voraciousness. They are trying to look threatening. Try to get in touch with your "inner grizzly bear" this week and notice things you do to subordinate your children and enhance your position of superiority over them.

Eliminate the following from your parenting repertoire:

- Pulling them by the arm
- Pulling them by the shirt collar
- Taking them by the wrist instead of the hand
- Towering over them to talk

- Touching their heads
- Tousling their hair
- Using a stern tone of voice
- Using a loud voice
- Crossing your arms or placing them on your hips
- Tightening your face and jaw
- Pushing them away
- Smacking a reaching hand
- Carrying them carpet style
- Tapping your toe in impatience
- Giving them the evil eye

Then you can moderate your body language to show more good will and to communicate you seek peace by making these alterations.

INSTEAD OF:	TRY:
Yelling across the house	Move right over to where your child is
Speaking loudly	Use a regular voice or speak even
Using a baritone	softer
	Speak in sweet soprano tones (not patronizing)
Standing over them	Squat down to eye level

How much less of a warrior are you going to look if you come into your child's bedroom and sit on the floor, lean back on the edge of the bed and get comfy with your arms resting over bent knees? These are very gentle and relaxed statements that show you are present and calm. You can gesture for them to come join you by patting the floor beside you. Then you might put your arm around your child and ask about what she had in mind for getting the driveway shoveled as she had promised. Chances are you'll elicit a more co-operative response than shouting up from the foyer, "Hey what's the deal with the driveway? You said you'd shovel it!"

The Power of Touch

Once you have got a handle on choosing body language that projects the message that you are a friend not a foe, then you might try to incorporate some kind of touch. The experience of touching others releases endorphins in the brain that are actually more powerful than morphine. If you want to get relaxed and stop those fight-or-flee chemicals, let's switch on the relaxing neural pathways.

You can rub your child's back while you talk, clasp her hand in yours and rub your thumb gently over her thumb. Even a touch of the hand to the shoulder is very connecting and loving. Your touch doesn't need to linger. Touch and release is still better than no contact at all. See if they'll accept it (if not – that's okay too). It's so powerful. In fact touch is so powerful a connector, that in controlled studies, it's been shown that waitresses can actually increase their tips by as much as 7 percent by touching the patron on the shoulder for two to four seconds when delivering the bill to the table.

Gentle touch should help break the cycle of "bracing" ourselves to deal with our children, which sets up a "chicken-and-egg" scenario. Which came first? Did you get your hackles up because your son walked towards the car with that specific strut he uses when something is bugging him? Or was your response brittle when he asked you to open the trunk to put his gym bag in? Who knows who sets off who first, but *you* can decide to do *your* part in actively changing your body language to counter any possible confusion.

The Right Words

While body language makes up the vast majority of our communication, we still can improve the 7 percent, which is the content of what we say. Often parents who have power issues with their children have a *style* of communication that is problematic. Here are the most common things to watch for:

STYLE OF COMMUNICATING	EXAMPLE
Blaming	"Well, if you didn't leave your bike on the driveway, this wouldn't happen."
Criticizing	"That's not how you load the dishwasher; don't put that glass there."
Humiliating	"Why do you always have to be such a problem?"
Lecturing	"I've had it with you; when are you gonna shape up? You don't seem to get it, do you? How many times do I have to go over this with you . . . ?"
Moralizing	"You know, it's not nice to be jealous of your sister. You're better than that. You should go say *sorry*."
Ordering	"Bring me my purse; watch your brother; pick that up; put that down."
Judging	"I think you could have done better. You don't seem to care about your studies. You don't seem to care about much, actually."

In times of conflict, we use our words as weapons. This artillery promotes aggression and that means the precious mutual respect that is required for co-operation goes right out the window.

• •

" . . . respect is like air. If you take it away, it is all people can think about. The instant people perceive disrespect in a conversation, the interaction is no longer about the original purpose—it is now about defending dignity."

—Patterson, Grenny, McMillan and Switzler
in *Crucial Conversations: Tools
for Talking When Stakes Are High*

• •

If we want to stay on topic and not get sidestepped into defending dignity, we have to watch our language content. It must be respectful.

Here are some communication rules and tools to use that maintain respect:

1. **If you don't have something nice to say, say nothing at all.**

   I am not joking! I'll continue to discuss how to incorporate positive communications in the chapters ahead, but at least let's put a halt on some of that nasty stuff that we let slip out without much thinking. I'm passionate about this advice. Our words are such a huge contributor to discouragement. In my first parenting class, the instructor, Althea Poulos, gave us the following homework: "Don't say anything negative to your children this week. Feel free to act if you need to; move them away from pushing the TV buttons, or take something from their hands."

   Who knew? I urge you to try this for yourself for one week. It's like the breakfast cereal challenge: "See for yourself— in just one week."

2. **Ask instead of telling.**

   It's more empowering to be asked than ordered around or reminded. Young children respond especially well to being asked. They *love* giving you the answer, and then you can acknowledge them for knowing so much. Older children feel respected when you are approaching them with a curious inquiry rather than an accusation. Here are some examples:

Younger Children

INSTEAD OF TELLING:	TRY ASKING:
It's time to go to school.	Hey, what time is it? (That's right! It's time to go school. You really know our morning routine.)
Clean up your toys.	What has to happen before we leave our play date? (Tidy up, that's right. You are very polite company to have over.)
Pick up your coat.	Where do coats need to be kept? (On the hooks, that's right. You sure help keep our house looking tidy.)

Older Children

INSTEAD OF TELLING:	TRY ASKING:
Turn off the TV; it's homework time.	What's your plan for getting your homework done?
Hey, get that garbage out!	What's your strategy for dealing with the garbage this week?

3. **Acknowledge that you can't force, and ask for a favor instead.**

   It's amazing how quickly you can dissolve a power struggle simply by communicating to your children that you do respect their power. If we let them know that we understand that we can't make them, and instead request their assistance, they often become co-operative almost immediately.

   It's as if they are trying to say: "Thank you very much for honoring the fact that I do have the power to totally ruin your morning. Now that you realize my power, I am all too happy to *volunteer* myself to the cause. Just don't *mandate* me!" Here are some examples:

u're right, I can't make you hurry up this morning, but I do need a favor. Would you be willing to help your old man? I am worried about being late for my first morning meeting at the office, and I could really use some help getting out the door on time. Can we do a quick scramble to get ready?"

- "I know I can't make you clean up, but I'd sure be grateful if you could tackle getting a few of those puzzles picked up before lunch."

- "Would you be willing to help us out by bringing your plate to the counter? Thank you!"

4. **Describe what you see.**

This one is so simple that everyone can put it into place immediately, and it will save you (and your kids) so much wasted time.

Instead of saying: "What is wrong with you? Are you a pig? Do you have no common sense? You left your towel on the bathroom floor, where it will become moldy. You have no respect for property, do you know that?" try: "I see a wet towel on the floor."

An observation (and nothing more) will prove far more effective than a lecture. One great catch-all phrase that falls into this category is, "I see you have a job to do." I recommend you try using this line whenever you see something that is the child's responsibility to look after. Often our children will try to egg us on into a fight by doing something slightly destructive in order to provoke a reaction from us. But this reply shows we are not taking the bait, and we are not willing to fight. It also leaves the responsibility where it belongs: on the child. They know it; we don't have to lecture.

So, if Chris dumps the dog's bowl over, sending kibbles 'n' bits across the entire kitchen, you can keep going about your business and comment, "I see you have a job to do." It's the child's job, not yours. So step over the kibbles, and don't say anything more about them until they're cleaned up. That means no nagging or reminding. However, when it's time for a bath, dinner or a video, you can respond with "Yes! . . . when you're jobs are done." Your kids will catch on after only a few weeks that each time they create a mess, eventually they have to get around to cleaning it up. They will also cease using behaviors that involve making more work for them and pulling your chain.

5. **Say it in a word.**

   I have a minimalist rule: Don't say in 10 words what can be said in 5, and don't say in 5 words what you can say in 1. Cut through the verbiage and just get to it! Your children understand when you say things like:

   - "Hands." (As they approach the table for supper, they know that means "Wash your hands before supper.")
   - "Boots." (In the front foyer, after tobogganing, they know that means put wet boots on the mat.)

6. **Lighten up.**

   Here is a law of life: You can't be fighting and laughing with someone at the same time.

   If you want to send a message of peace, try getting silly for a few moments. It will lighten the mood and make way for easier times ahead.

   If Ray refuses to put on his boots, try putting his boot on your head. "Hey, Ray, do you think I look good in my new hat?" Once you are both laughing together, the chances of the resistance ending and co-operation proceeding are greatly improved. If nothing else, it will cheer you up.

If we can get our body language and word content to be less domineering, we are more likely to have our children respond non-defensively to us. However, the greatest tool for ending a power struggle is to stop pushing our agenda, and instead listen to our children's points of view.

Listening Instead of Talking

Brain researchers have confirmed that it is impossible to multitask. We can be attentive to one channel of thought only. Now yes, we can jump back and forth between two channels very quickly, but we can't actually attend to two channels simultaneously.

When we are fighting, the feeling that we need to defend ourselves is so great it can make it impossible to listen to the other person. As soon as he or she attacks, we stop listening and start composing our comeback.

Usually we tune out the other person and instead of listening we get our lips flapping and that usually means verbal assaults that only make matters worse.

While I have offered some body language and talking tips, communication is not only about getting our message across; it's also about receiving our children's messages. It's an exchange that includes listening.

Author Stephen Covey in his book *The Seven Habits of Highly Effective Families* urges us to "seek first to understand and then be understood." That is generally a twist for parents, who feel they are wise and that children must be made to understand them: "If they only understood why I want them to eat the blasted salad at dinner, or put their coat on for school, they'd see my brilliance and this problem would be solved. I better keep convincing them."

However, if we want to offer the olive branch, we are going to have to show in words and actions that we are here to listen, not to push our agenda. That is how we will learn that our daughter would be happy to eat cooked vegetables instead of raw salad greens, and that Sam doesn't want to wear a coat to school because it's too bulky to run in at recess—he always loses at tag. It turns out, if Sam brings a coat to school, the teacher makes him wear it, but if he doesn't bring one, she lets him go without. His friends without coats are winning at tag every day!

Just think of all the things you'll learn when you start listening. If you can hold a place in your toolbox for the art of listening, we'll discuss the how-to's of it in the next chapter, but they certainly apply here, too.

P: Plow on Positively

Part of what maintains a power struggle is our insistence on changing our child's behavior. "Oh goodness," we tell ourselves, "life would be just fine, if *you* would only . . . (do something differently)."

If YOU would just eat.

If YOU would just do your homework.

If YOU would just pick up after yourself.

If YOU would stop forgetting.

If YOU would do something different—then this problem would go away. It's all *you*, kiddo.

Boy, you're really counting on your children. In fact, you're actually *dependent* on them, because by your current way of thinking, your children are the only ones able to change the situation. Not only do we have to shift the power, but we also have to shift our attention away from them, and back onto ourselves. What things can *we* be doing to influence the situation? It's our job to manage our responsibilities and to stop micromanaging how others handle theirs.

> *Jenny is in Grade Four and is very forgetful. Everyday Mom has to check her backpack to make sure Jenny has her home-work and agenda and lunch before going to school. Every day at pick-up time, Mom goes to Jenny's locker and makes sure she hasn't left anything behind and double-checks to see that she has brought her mitts and things home. Mom has to stay on Jenny's case constantly to manage these things. They often fight about where things are and why Jenny is not more organized. Mom believes if she didn't do it, Jenny could never remember.*

Is it that Jenny *can't* or *won't* manage her things? Mom has made such a big issue out of Jenny and her disorganization that it has become a power struggle. To Jenny, looking after her things will feel like losing to Mom. If Mom drops the rope and no power dynamics are in play, Jenny could begin to make a change in her ways without feeling conquered. Mom can do this by changing her attitudes and actions. When Mom realizes it's a power struggle, then stops and re-assesses the situation, she sees it's the responsibility of Jenny to do these tasks. Mom can let Jenny know this. "Jenny, I realize that I have been micromanaging your responsibilities with school, and I see now that it was disrespectful of me to think you couldn't man-age. From now on, I trust you to look after getting your things to and from school, and I won't mention that again. I apologize for underestimating you." Now Mom's actions are to *stop* rescuing and *stop* overstepping her boundaries. She's showing faith in Jenny to figure out what she needs to do for herself. She is trusting Jenny to learn to manage her life. Mom's responsibilities are to pick her up and drop her off at school. In the mornings, Mom can spend her time looking after her own duties of getting ready for the day and, yes, having a peaceful cup of coffee.

Jenny will test. That's to be expected. There may well be a few weeks of mistakes; perhaps there will be homework left at school, missing mittens and some other chaos. However, these are Jenny's problems to figure out, and she will! Faced with a detention for not having work completed, and needing to keep her hands in her pockets for warmth when playing outside at recess, suddenly Jenny starts seeing the merits of paying extra attention to her responsibilities. It's new to her, since Mom did these jobs before, but after some initial struggles she will get it. She'll creatively find solutions to help her manage her responsibilities. All the while, she experiences a new reaction from Mom. Mom now believes in Jenny's ability to figure things out for herself: "I am sorry you lost a few marks for your late assignment. That must have been disheartening; I am sure you'll figure it out for next time." Gee, now Jenny hears that her Mom thinks she is a pretty capable girl, and she likes that feeling. After a few weeks and slip-ups Jenny realizes that she manages her responsibilities well. She is growing up! That is how Jenny will now feel capable—one of her Crucial C's—rather than feeling demeaned by Mom and then proving her strength by yanking her mother's chain.

Here is another example of plowing on positively:

Every evening Dad screams at the boys to get ready for karate lessons. "We'll be late! Let's go!" They poke about and take their sweet time, while Dad's blood pressure is skyrocketing. But wait just a minute. Whose activity is this? The boys'. Whose responsibility is it to be punctual then? The boys'. Dad's responsibility is to pay for the lessons and to drive them. Dad can stop micromanaging the boys' responsibility of watching the clock and instead get on with the part of the job he agreed to: driving. Dad can let the boys know: "Karate is your activity, and I am willing to be the driver, but not the clock-watcher. Please call me when you are ready for me to drive you and I trust you'll manage the rest."

With the responsibilities clearly defined, and Dad concerning himself only with his business, the fights stop and the boys learn to get themselves ready on time. Go figure.

Dexter (three years old) dawdles in the family room, resisting tuck-in time by acting like he can't hear his mother at all. He just keeps playing with his trucks never looking up. Mom waits at the doorway shouting, "Let's go, Pokie! Come on, it's late. I don't want another bad tuck-in like last night. You better come now. I don't want this to end in tears." She sees she is in for another struggle and starts putting on her fighting armor—a terse tone, staunch body language and an inflexible non-humorous attitude.

I bet you 10 bucks that tooth brushing and PJs are a nightmare to Dexter's family. The opponents seem poised to fight. Instead of Mom being stuck waiting for Dexter who won't follow her orders, she could simply announce *her plans* and get busy with *her responsibilities*: "Dexter, I am starting tuck-ins" and head upstairs herself. Believe it or not, Dexter is more likely to scramble up after her than he is to lead the way, just because she has said it's time for bed. Mom whistles her way merrily to Dexter's room and calls down, "I am available for help with PJs if you're interested." After a few moments she can move to the washroom. "It's tooth brushing time—any takers?" Finally, after a few minutes, Mom can leave the washroom, lay on Dexter's bed and start reading *Goldilocks and the Three Bears* aloud. Once the story is over, Mom's responsibilities are complete. She goes downstairs to say to Dexter, "Tuck-in time is over; it's time to be in your room. Can you come on your own, or do you need to be carried?" Then, if needed, Mom carries Dexter lovingly to bed, kisses him and leaves. He may choose to put on his PJs and brush his teeth, but that is up to him. There are no tuck-in stories or songs, because he chose to miss that part of the evening. That is his right. The train was leaving the station and he didn't get on board. He can choose differently tomorrow night. And don't worry, he will.

THE ROPE IS DROPPED: NOW LET'S PROBLEM SOLVE

The DROP model helps to disengage us from the fight. It's not exactly a step-by-step process so much as a holistic, attitudinal re-arrangement. We can cease being the oppositional force that our child wants to rail against. When we are no longer trying to win, we can get into the deeper more constructive business of power shifting through creating choices and solving problems.

Choice, Choice and More Choice

"Which would you like? You decide!"

If you have choice, the power sits with you. The parent of a power-seeking child needs to be thinking all the time about how to help the child be more self-directed and self-determined. If we can keep up with this ever-changing target, we can avoid power struggles.

Heck, your children probably grew and developed just in the last 24 hours, but when was the last time you altered your viewpoint about them? We have to do a better job of moving responsibility and control over to our children on an ongoing basis. We can do this by expanding their choices. The more choices they have, the more empowered they are.

With choices, our kids will have the opportunity to say, "YES! I decide for me," which helps counter their perception that we are trying to control them. Get those creative juices flowing. Think about how you might add an element of choice in any situation.

I already hear your objection: "Well there is NO choice about brushing your teeth—that *has* to be done." I know we have to work towards getting teeth brushed, but the fighting, inflexibility and insistence on doing it your way (the only way, the right way) is creating resistance.

We can take that barricade down by offering choice and allowing the child do some decision-making. This stimulates the desire to choose tooth brushing. "The plaque eats away at our teeth, so we need to brush it off to keep our teeth healthy. . . . Would you like to brush first or shall I?" Here are some other suggestions:

- "We need to brush for bedtime; do you want to do it before or after PJs are on?"
- "Do you want to brush with toothpaste? Or do you want to floss and rinse with an oral rinse?"
- "We need to keep the plaque from building on our teeth. I see I can't make you brush, that is your decision, but if we want the freedom to eat foods that leave harmful stuff on our teeth, like milk and juice and sweets, then we have to be responsible for brushing if off. The other choice is not to eat those foods that hurt our teeth so we don't have to worry so much about tooth decay. You decide."

Common Parenting Pitfall: Watch What they DO (not what they say)

Children inform you of their decision by what they do, not by what they say. If your child tells you she will brush her teeth, but then doesn't, she is making a decision. As she leaves the washroom, you can say, "I see you've decided no sweets tomorrow." Just be sure you stay firm and friendly in following through with the no-sugar day. Firm means no sugar. Friendly means no lecturing about how if she had done what she was supposed to do. . . . When your child freaks on you because the next day she can't have her fruit roll-up, simple empathize and say, "I am sorry you're unhappy with your decision. You can choose differently for yourself tonight."

Common Parenting Pitfall: Acting Like You Don't Care (but secretly you want them to make *your* choice!)

"Alyson, I tried that and it didn't work. He didn't brush or eat sweets for a month!" Here's what I say to that: "A *month*! Wow, something is going wrong. If your child is still not brushing, or your toddler is still walking around in a poopy diaper, or what have you, THE POWER STRUGGLE IS STILL ON."

You can end the overt fighting but the two parties can still be locked in their positions unwilling to move and let the other win. Somehow your child is still under the impression you want him to change and do things your way. Ask yourself if you are really being bi-partisan and friendly? Or do you sound more like this, "Are you going to brush your teeth tonight? No? Well, you know what that means, no juice for you tomorrow, missy. No whining to me about it. It's your choice, not mine. I don't want to hear about this tomorrow, do you understand?"

The idea of offering choice is to free children to decide, allowing them to experience the outcomes of their choices and understanding that with the absence of manipulation, they will most likely fall closely in line and live co-operatively. If we insert our personal power into the exercising of choice, we muck it all up. I have yet to work with a child who has the goal of power who didn't have a power parent.

You can find choice in any situation once you get good at it. Even a diabetic child who needs insulin shots will feel more in control of himself and the situation if given a choice. "Would you like to have your needle in the right or left thigh?" A youngster who doesn't like taking her yucky-tasting medicine can be given the power to decide if she would like to order the bubble gum- or the banana-flavored penicillin. She can decide if she would like to take it now or after her TV show is over. We help improve matters by injecting choice into sticky situations where co-operation is difficult and where power struggles typically erupt.

This is a power-shifting strategy. As our children grow and develop, they must take on more responsibility and control of their own lives. We need to keep expanding the choices they can make for themselves to help launch them into adulthood. Here is one simple example of expanding choice with age and ability:

No Choice: "Here is your sippy cup."
Limited Choice: "Would you like apple or orange juice in your sippy cup?"
Full Choice: "What would you like to drink?"
Autonomy: "Help yourself when you are thirsty. Cups are in the cupboard. You can look after that on your own now. You don't need my help—you're capable."

The amount of choice a child has should increase with age. If you are power struggling, you're holding on to choice options that your children are ready to make for themselves. It's hard not to infantilize our youth. These types of fights are our reminders that we are holding them back from growing. We have to let go.

In the next example, little Pauline grows up and is gradually offered more choice. Notice her budding autonomy and self-reliance, which helps provide the crucial C of becoming capable. In addition, as Pauline becomes marvelously talented at managing herself, she is directed away from a self-interested mindset and pointed towards "supporting the team." Let's have a look:

No Choice: "Here is your dinner, Pauline."

Limited Choice: "Would you like to pick some vegetables to have with our supper?"

Full Choice: "Would you like to choose what the family eats for supper on Monday nights?"

Full Choice with Responsibility: "What would you like to learn to cook for us so you can make and serve the Monday meal?"

Autonomy: "Thanks for that great meal! It's so nice to come home to dinner being ready. I'll do the dishes; the cook has already done the hard work."

Common Parenting Pitfall: Stuck by Their Refusal to Make a Choice

I love the idea of offering choices, but when I ask Jules if he wants to have apple juice or orange juice, he doesn't answer. Now what am I supposed to do?

Jules, you smart boy! He is seeking power, and, boy, does he hold it in his silence. I recommend in these situations that you still offer choice:

"Would you like to decide on your juice, or shall I?"

If Jules still doesn't speak up with his choice, then his behavior states his choice (the choice is to have you decide) to which you can respond, "I see you would like me to decide. Okay, here is your apple juice."

Yes, yes, Jules will probably cry now because this was a power dance that made him feel big and you just changed your dance steps. "The time for deciding has come and gone. I can see you're disappointed. You can choose differently next time." Nothing else needs to be said. Move along to the next activity and don't dwell on the past.

POWER SHIFTING: LET ROUTINES BE THE BOSS

Another way of ensuring that we don't accidently come off looking like the family dictator, wielding power and expecting obedience, is to let the routines of the family be the boss. This is similar to looking to the needs of the situation for guidance. It allows us to say. "We do this because it's the routine of the family," rather than "because I say so."

As a parent, it's our job to establish and maintain the routines of the home to prevent chaos from erupting. Our children actually respond very well to having a structure. They appreciate having expectations, limits and boundaries. These are like the walls of a nest that make them feel safely hemmed in and protected.

Many power struggles erupt when we break from the routines, or when we think we have routines but we don't really. Let me give you an example:

Petra has always made it part of the daily routine to have the toy room cleaned up before supper. When the children were small, she would help them, showing them where things belonged on the shelf, and helping them place certain items in a big bin and other items on the shelf. The riding toys were parked in the corner, the connector set in a Tupperware container. The children eventually learned all about how to clean up, and so Petra handed this responsibility to them. "You know all there is to know about cleaning up your play area. You don't need my help or instruction anymore. From now on that is your job to do before supper."

The first night, they didn't want to do the cleanup. But Mom enforced this by stating the routine that they had been following for as long as they could remember: "When your play room is cleaned up, then I'll know it's time for dinner."

This is called a when/then statement, and it both empowers the child and states the routine as boss. Compare that statement to, "No dinner until that play room is cleaned up." The latter statement is a threat. Mom lords power over the children saying, "Do as I say or else. . . ."

Let's look at some more examples of excellent when/then statements:

- When your teeth are brushed, I'll know you're ready for juice.
- When your coat is on, I'll know you're ready to go out and build a snowman.
- When your crayons are picked up, I'll know you're ready for the next activity.
- When your job is done, I'll know you're ready for your video.
- When your room is all tidy, I'll know you're ready for company to come in.

Common Parenting Pitfall: Thinking You're Being Routine When You're Not

Talia and her mom are fighting. Talia wants to stay up; Mom says it's her bedtime. It's a power struggle, and Mom is determined to win because she has the best ammunition in her mind: it is late for a little growing girl (needs of the situation) and 8 p.m. is Talia's bedtime (let the routine be boss).

Why is this going off the rails? Well, it turns out that Talia's 8 p.m. bedtime exists only in Mother's mind. It is *not* the established routine. Mom tries to "aim" for 8 p.m., but if Talia is good company and Mom doesn't want to be alone because her partner is working the late shift, she keeps Talia up with her. However, if Talia is grumpy or if her partner is home in the evening, she sends Talia to bed, sometimes earlier, sometimes later.

Mom would be acting in ways that were more respectful to Talia and to the social order, if every evening the bedtime was the same. Regardless of Mom's need for company or Talia's mood, the deciding factor is the clock! No personal power, just a fact. It's 8 p.m., and that is bedtime. If Mom sticks to this routine, the fights will end and Talia won't negotiate bedtime. She will accept it as just the way things are, and it will become automatic.

Try it. Think about the area where most power struggles are created in your own home and ask yourself if you have properly established and enforced the routines that your children are to be following.

Common Parenting Pitfall: Gatekeeping

"Mommy, can you buy me this book?"

It's anybody's guess as to whether Mom will say yes or no to this request. A million thoughts race through your parenting brain when asked a question like this:

- Is it a book I like, too?
- When did I buy the last one?
- Is it under $20 and really doesn't count as a considerable purchase?
- What day does the mortgage payment come out?
- Do I feel generous today? Am I in a good mood?
- Did you make a fuss leaving kindergym this morning?
- Are you healthy? (Being sick helps with getting things bought for you—sympathy and all.)

Mom holds all of the power in this scenario. *She* decides yes or no. That is fine when our children are very young, but if we start to encounter power struggles, it's time to think things through again.

How do we keep our parenting authority without gatekeeping? Is there a way to hand this decision over to the child? Can we make our decision-making process more transparent so it doesn't feel so arbitrary?

It may be time to start an allowance that has books in the budget. Or, Mom might reveal that she is willing to buy two books a month. Now, at least, the child understands that when Mom says " no," it's not because of her personally kyboshing the request arbitrarily—she's just following the "two books a month" rule.

Ian used to fight with his dad every day at school. He didn't want to go home. He wanted to stay and play. Until he learned about gatekeeping and arbitrary power, Dad would fight, and sometimes he would win and they would go home.

Other times Ian would win and they would stay and play for a bit. Every day was a fight, though. After Dad saw that they had no routine for their play schedule and that he was acting as the gatekeeper, exerting arbitrary power, he made a change. Ian and Dad pulled out a calendar and made a plan to stay late at the school to play on Wednesdays and Fridays. On Mondays, Tuesdays and Thursdays they would go straight home. This worked out for both of them because the fights ended, and both Ian and Dad actually enjoyed their playtime more when they were both in the mood for it.

JOINT PROBLEM-SOLVING

Ian and Dad solved their problem! They stopped fighting and got to win/win. I can't stress enough how important it is for our children who are missing the crucial C of feeling capable to get to this step.

> If they won't eat salad—that is a problem that needs a solution.
>
> If they won't go to bed—that is a problem that needs a solution.
>
> If they won't brush their teeth—that is a problem that needs a solution.

If your children fight over your refusal to buy them a book or leaving the playground or cleaning up before dinner—WHATEVER!— these fights should all be viewed as family problems in need of a solution rather than a misbehavior that needs disciplinary action. It's a very different way to frame the situation in your mind.

When we get into our "policing" mindset, we tend to want to use logical consequences to correct the child's behavior. However, and I need you to get a highlighter and mark this page now: LOGICAL CONSEQUENCES are NOT a good tool for power struggles. They always come off wrong. It's too easy to look powerful when enacting a logical consequence—and besides, there are better tools.

Let me share a story I learned from Jane Nelson, author of the *Positive Discipline* series of books, which beautifully illustrates the difference:

A teacher was at her wit's end trying to get her students to be more punctual at recess. She spoke with the children. "Every day people are coming in late from recess and it's cutting into our instruction time. What would be a good punishment?" The children came up with things like:

- Write the pupils' names on the board.
- Send them to the principal's office for the afternoon.
- Make them write out, "I will not be late coming in from recess," 100 times.
- Make them clean the blackboard brushes.

The teacher in the next room didn't believe in punishment, but he too had troubles with his children coming in on time at recess. He asked his students, "What is a good logical consequence for being late coming in from recess?" The students offered:

- Stay in after school.
- Miss that many minutes the next recess.
- Take that many minutes off our gym class.

A third teacher put this issue on the agenda to be discussed with her students during their weekly classroom meeting. During the meeting, the teacher said, "I have a problem I need some help with. I have only so many minutes of instruction time each day. People are getting in late from the recess bell and so it cuts into my teaching time. How can we do this better? Does anyone have any ideas for solving this problem?"

Posed as a problem that the teacher was having, and presented during a time of peace, the children volunteered very different answers:

- The bell is very quiet, and when you are playing soccer in the field, you can't really hear it that well. You don't know it has rung till you look up and notice that everyone is going in. Can you ask them to turn up the bell?
- What if the schoolyard monitor carried a hand bell, and when the school bell rings, they walked to the edge of the tarmac and started ringing the bell so we could hear it?
- What if we did the same thing as we do in frozen tag where each person becomes "it" and spreads the word to the next person that the bell has rung?
- What if recess was longer so we could get a whole game in, and then lunch was shorter? You just get outside and you have to come back in!

Wow, hey? There is big difference in the types of answers you generate from children when you ask the question differently. I think it's clear that asking for solutions to problems is much more powerful at getting to the heart of the matter. Children have so much to contribute if we are willing to listen. Our children are willing to live within the rules they help to establish. It empowers them, and it stimulates co-operation.

My own children and I had a problem with them leaving their socks in the family room. A punishment would be to yell about it, a consequence might be to confiscate the socks so they can't find them. But instead I asked, "How can we solve this?"

My girls said they didn't like going all the way upstairs to their bedroom to put their socks in the laundry hamper, but they suggested that if they had a little basket in the mudroom, they could take them off and leave them in the basket there instead of in the family room. They'd take them up to their room on one of their trips upstairs later in the evening or later that week. BRAVO! I don't have to find smelly socks in the couch cushions and they don't have to make that extra trip upstairs. Brilliant.

What better training for everyone in your family to learn how to get along than joint problem-solving? Instead of one person dominating, we seek a truly equitable solution that does not belittle or tyrannize anyone. Our children will learn skills of co-operation that will help them get along with their classmates, friends, colleagues, and in their intimate relationships and families of their own. Healthy, respectful relationships with proper power balances allow us to be tightly connected and enriched. What a gift to give our children.

Let's look next at the child with the mistaken goal of revenge and see what happens if we don't successfully solve the power issues in our family.

CHAPTER SIX
REVENGE

When Diane went to load groceries into the backseat of her car, she was shocked and horrified to discover that the leather seat had been peed on. Earlier that day she had a fight with Wyatt over all the toys and wrapper mess he had made in the backseat, and she forced him to clean up his side. She was particularly frustrated because his brother was able to keep his side of the car neat and tidy—clearly this wasn't about a lack of ability or not being taught how to keep a space tidy. She pointed this out to Wyatt, "Look at your brother's side. He is always so tidy. Why can't you be?"

It seems he cleaned his mess alright, but left a "little something" for Mother to let her know just exactly how he feels. Wyatt thinks, "I'll never be as good as my brother in my mom's eyes, but why must she constantly rub my nose in it?"

Wyatt's goal was to seek revenge and hurt his mother as he felt hurt by her. It worked! But, he isn't a "bad seed." He's discouraged, just like Lewis in the story below.

Lewis' teacher accused him of roughing up another boy and sent him to the principal's office. It was the third time that week he had sat on those chairs outside the office where every passerby noticed that there is something wrong with him. On the way, Lewis stopped in the boys' room and clogged up one of the toilets with paper hand towels. "Everyone in this school hates me. Well guess what? It's mutual." he justified to himself as he flushed another wad down.

Lewis and Wyatt are two hurtin' kids. They want to believe they are better than the way people see them. Somehow they can't find their way out of the trap they are in. In their anger and hurt, they lash out and retaliate. They "even the score" because the alternative is to accept being degraded. They find their crucial C of proving they count by reacting to their perceived mistreatment. The retaliation protects their ego from the assaults they experience. But it has cost them their reputations, and they have been cast in roles that make people expect the worst from them. Guess what? They deliver. Abhorrent behaviors abound.

In this chapter we're on a mission to change the way we deal with children who are trying to prove they count through the mistaken goal of revenge.

PRESCRIPTION FOR REVENGE: STOP INFLICTING PAIN AND HEAL THE HURT

Since children who seek revenge never strike first, it's a fairly straightforward prescription for change: stop the hurting and help the healing. This is your last call folks: if you have been using punishment as your parenting method, it's *really* time to stop. No more.

However, hurt can come from many varied sources. Parents are often shocked to learn the ways our children feel hurt in our families. They often have no idea! Here are some of the biggest culprits that contribute to your child's hurt and that you should be alerted to:

1. Being punished
2. Losing power struggles
3. Perceiving sibling favoritism

We will explore the major ways that we can lessen feelings of favoritism in our houses:

- Stop being "fair"
- Free your children from their roles
- Learn new ways to respond to sibling conflict without siding with one child:
  * ignore it
  * put them in the same boat
  * put it on the agenda
  * the two-arm technique (no, it's a not wrestling move)
  * bugs and wishes

Finally, we'll learn some new parenting skills, too:

- The skill of active listening
- Actions to help heal and re-build the relationship

And, of course, I'll continue to inform you of the common mistakes parents make in the application of these tools, so you can stay ahead of the learning curve.

WHY PUNISHMENT DOESN'T WORK

Punishment hurts. The fact that it hurts is the very mechanism that supposedly makes it effective. But *hello*! We know it is not working because we have a hurting child who is retaliating instead of "reforming" (are you loving social equality yet?).

I have argued this point since the beginning of the book. Our children have the same ability to feel pain and hurt as an adult. They don't have an inferior nervous system or a deficiency in their emotional center that makes them somehow immune to parental admonishments. Our children feel just as we feel, and they thrive when treated with respect and dignity, just as we do. So the golden rule applies: treat others (your children) the same way you want to be treated. It's not a tough rule to understand. It's doing it that can be surprisingly difficult, especially when parenting. Don't worry: we will fill you up with more non-punitive tools in this chapter.

However, maybe you still cling to the idea that pain is somehow remedial. Does it bother you that Jill is having too much fun vacuuming up the potting soil she purposely spilled? Do you find yourself wishing she was upset, or do you feel like since she is enjoying the clean up you are somehow rewarding bad behavior? We have to get these ideas 100 percent out of our minds if we are to make progress. For starters, keep chanting: "Children who feel good, do good; children who feel bad, do bad."

All punishment must cease. Not just the blatant corporal punishment of spanking, hitting, pinching and any other such physical assaults: I am appealing to you to eliminate any of those "make them feel bad" strategies you may employ. We have to let go of all our negative body language that is attempting to cause some form of ache or upset in our children. The rolling eyeballs that say, "You disgust me." The crossed arms that say, "I've had enough of you." Ouch Ouch Ouch. STOP.

My Abbreviated Checklist of Things to STOP doing:

1. **Stop using hurtful words:**

   "What's wrong with you, anyway?"

   "You're driving me nuts, do you know that?"

   "I am sick of you and you're carrying on; just stop it!"

   "He's my little monster child."

   "You sure know how to ruin things."

   "Why do I even bother with you?"

   "Smarten up!"

2. **Stop sending hurtful messages—things we don't dare say out loud, but if we feel them, so do our children. These unspoken messages are in the subtext of our communications:**

   "You're not good enough."

   "You're a problem."

   "I don't love you."

   "You're a liability to my life."

   "My life would be better if I didn't have to deal with you."

   "You'll never amount to anything."

   "You aren't the child I wanted."

   "Our family would have been perfect if not for you."

   "You ruin everything."

   "You'll never amount to anything."

3. **Stop hurtful actions:**

   - Hitting with belts, spoons, hair brushes (Yes, it gets worse, but I think you get the idea.)
   - Spanking
   - Smacking hands
   - Swatting bums
   - Pinching

- Forcing the child to stand against a wall with arms overhead
- Carrying the child aggressively or tugging on shirt collars or wrists
- Sending the child to bed without dinner
- Forcing the child into confinement and isolation ("Go to your room!")
- Withholding allowance ("That'll be a dollar docked for every cuss word, mister.")
- Withholding love (stonewalling, rejection, silent treatment)
- Forced labor ("Just for that, you'll be pulling dandelions from the lawn this weekend.")
- Confiscating possessions ("If you can't treat your brother nicely, I am taking your Yugio cards away.")
- Removing privileges ("With that kind of rudeness, you can plan on no television this week. If I hear another peep, it's two weeks with no TV!")
- Humiliation and shaming tactics ("Look in my eyes. Look at me when I'm talking. Now say what I told you back to me . . . say it." "Are you a little boy? Do little boys need to sit in little highchairs again and wear diapers like a little baby does? Well, you're crying liking a baby." "Go sit on your naughty chair until you can behave.")
- Token economy systems ("I'll give you a marble for good behavior, but I'll take away a marble for bad behavior. You didn't make your bed this morning so that was a three-marble infraction.")
- Sarcasm ("Look at this report card. Well, I guess we don't need to be putting away money for a Harvard education.")

When the child's goal is revenge, our parenting job is to help the hurting child heal. You are only getting in the way of your own goal when you punish. Think about what would be helpful to you if you were hurting. If your family discounted you, would more punishment make you shape up? Or would loving kindness be more apt to bring about a softening of your counterattacks? We have to find ways to replenish our children's crucial sense that they count in our families. It's a necessary condition for co-operation to occur.

• •

The floggings will continue until the morale improves.

• •

The difficulty in dealing with children who seek revenge is that they often behave in ways that make it harder to *want to* act in loving and kind ways towards them, but I know you can see behind their tough façade now. Once they feel safe and secure again, when they don't need to lob back the cannons we've been throwing, we will begin to see more of the soft and loving nature that is in each and every one of our children. There are non-punitive tools peppered throughout every chapter so that parents can trade in an old punitive technique for a new, positive discipline alternative.

STOP WINNING POWER STRUGGLES

We know from the last chapter on power that our best parenting approach is to dissolve power struggles, drop the rope, have a truce, and work towards win-win solutions.

Up till now, we often ended power struggles by winning them and defeating our children. Repeated defeat hurts. If the power balance has been skewed for a while, the child is most likely harboring resentment, and that hurt will be expressed in acts of

revenge. Healing old deep wounds can take time. Be patient with
your hurt child.

It's not just the fact that we were winning power struggles for so
long, but also *how* we were winning: by using those darned punishments. Lets face it, when our back is up against the wall and matters
are escalating, we just start pulling out bigger and bigger weapons
in order to win. Sometimes we use overt and blatant punishment,
but other times it's not so easy to see how we were being punitive.
There are those "tricky hidden punishments" that are harder to
recognize, even though we're the ones using them. Being calm and
not screaming is no guarantee we aren't being punitive. We can
seem oh-so-reasonable. We can convince ourselves that we are not
in a fight and that we are simply following through with democratic
principles (We tell ourselves, of course they don't like it and that is
why they are spitting at me and saying "I hate you!").

But, are you *sure* you're being democratic? A revenge-seeking
child tells us differently. Maybe our calmness is coming off as
cold-blooded or even cruel.

> *"Get off the computer, Braydon. That is enough computer for*
> *one night." Braydon hears his mom, but his friends are still*
> *IM'ing about plans for the weekend and Braydon doesn't want*
> *to miss out. Usually, if he ignores her, he can squeeze an extra*
> *ten minutes in. When Braydon keeps IM'ing, Mom unplugs the*
> *computer from the wall announcing, "That's it . . . I'm taking*
> *it away if you can't turn it off when you are told." She smiles*
> *at Braydon and calmly walks off with his laptop under her*
> *arm. "Take that," she thinks to herself.*

Braydon is apoplectic. Mom might as well have cut off his hand
and killed his social life in one fell swoop.

Mom convinces herself that she is confiscating his computer as a "logical consequence," so she can justify her actions. "If freedoms and responsibilities go hand in hand, then it is logical that if you don't use the computer properly, you lose your freedoms and the computer is taken away. Isn't this the new respectful egalitarian way?"

Sure, she can make it hold up rationally in her head, but that doesn't stop it from being punitive.

- Mom holds power over Braydon because she is still expecting him to "jump" on her command. (He must log off whenever she randomly decides it's enough. This is very ambiguous and smacks of gatekeeping.)

- There is no pre-set agreement or well-disclosed expectation about how much computer time Braydon is entitled to each night. He often gets extra time by ignoring her requests to shut it down. Why should tonight be any different?

- Mom didn't reveal the consequence of losing the computer in advance. She threatens often, but Braydon knows these are idle threats Mom doesn't follow through on. She has taught him that.

- What were Mom's intentions? Mom took the computer away as a tactic to win and get her way, but also to make him pay for not listening to her. She is not trying to teach and stimulate his co-operation about his computer use. She has not only ambitions to WIN but also to HURT him for his actions. She wants him to feel regret and remorse, but he's one of those modern resistant kids who feels his equality, so instead, he feels hurt and will seek revenge.

Common Parenting Pitfall: Using "Mock Consequences" to Disguise Your Punishment

Using mock consequences to win fights is not the same as dissolving power struggles or being firm and friendly. If parents continue to enter into power struggles, fight with their children and win by triumphing with punishments that hurt their children, there is going to be some form of revenge to face eventually. After all, how many times can you cut a person down without it taking a toll? To fight and lose repeatedly to your parents is to live in a state of oppression.

Rebellion reveals a desire to win power.
Revenge is in the business of hurting.

Braydon doesn't see his mom's taking his computer away as being logical. To him, it was an act of cruelty. It's the intention to hurt him that sets Mom up to be the target of his revenge. We need to get Mom to stop giving Braydon reasons to want to get back at her.

So, an important reminder: stop winning power struggles, and keep a keen eye out for any bogus "logical" consequence. In fact, instead of consequences, I urge you to move along to mutual problem-solving tactics that I recommend as the preferred tool for power struggles. Jeremy and Mom need to figure out how to manage the computer situation together. I'll be discussing this again in Chapter 8 when we talk about holding family meetings.

PERCEPTIONS OF FAVORITISM BY BIRTH ORDER

When I am looking for what might be the source of a hurt in a revengeful child, I take a good look at the other siblings. How does a revengeful child fit into the whole constellation of the family, and how do things generally play out at home for him or her?

Since the number one source of discouragement for our children is the perception that another sibling is preferred, I have a good hunch that we'll find the culprit here.

••

The biggest source of discouragement for our children is the perception that another sibling is preferred.

••

It Sucks Being Me in This Family!

The grass is always greener on the other side of the fence, isn't it? Each child in the family has a unique vantage point from which to observe the family, usually while throwing crabapples at siblings because *they* have it better! There is no actual better or worse birth order; it's all in the child's perception. But if we could see family life through a child's eyes, we'd see why each of our children *might* feel they are being short-shrifted.

Why It Sucks to Be the Eldest

- Mom and Dad put the pressure on me to set a good example for my younger sibs.
- I am forced to include my younger siblings. Why does Sally have to tag along with us to the movies? We want to meet boys!
- I am treated like a built-in babysitter.
- I get asked to do more because I am more capable and more responsible.

- I am expected to share or acquiesce to my younger sibs since "they don't understand."
- Everything gets dumbed-down to their level. I have to watch cartoons instead of *Friends*. In the car, I can't listen to the radio. I have to listen to *The Wiggles* instead. ("Oh, come on! Not *The Wiggles* again! Who signed me up for this? You care more about my sisters than me! I always have to give in to them.")

Ouch, hurt! That is tough. Who would want to be an eldest? Wouldn't it be better to be the middle child then?

Why It Sucks More to Be a Middle Child

- I don't get any of the privileges of the eldest, *nor* the pampering of the baby—I get nothing.
- I feel squeezed out of my family. I get more attention at my friends' houses than my own.
- I always have to be the middle man in fights and mediate everything.
- I don't feel special in anyway, and I'm not best at anything. I don't stand out; I fade away.
- I live in the shadow of my elder sibling who seems to do everything Mom and Dad want. How can I keep up with that?
- I don't feel understood. No one sees things from my perspective.
- I get blamed more than anyone else. That feels so unfair.
- I feel like my role in the family is to be "the problem." I always seem to be the one that Mom and Dad take issue with.

- I feel everything is harder for me and people are harder on me.
- People never cut me a break like they do with my siblings.

Gee, and you thought the eldest had it bad. You can see why "That's not FAIR!" is the middle child's battle cry and why she fights for the rights of the underdog.

Why Being the Baby in the Family Sucks Too

- I don't have anyone younger than me to push around.
- You guys get to do everything first: you got to go to school first, you get allowance first, you go to camp and sleepovers first. I want to try too, but I am told, "No, you're too young; you have to wait."
- By the time *I* do something for the first time, it's not new to Mom and Dad anymore. It's like they don't care that I'm learning to ride a bike, but they gave you a ticker-tape parade and made a movie. How is that supposed to make me feel?
- Everything you do is bigger and better. Bigger ski hills, bigger bike, harder math. I am reminded of my smallness and inabilities at every turn.
- I feel laughed at when I slip up. I feel hurt when you say I am stupid because I asked if those were real gnomes on the front lawn. That is not a silly question. I mean if there is a tooth fairy, couldn't those be real too? I *do so* have important thoughts, you know!
- I ask for new things, and I am told to use your scuffed-up hand-me-downs, and I don't even like the color. Can't I have something for myself? Don't I count?

- I would do anything to be like you and be included in your play, even if that means you dress me up like a cat, tie me up in skipping rope and laugh at me. I am willing to be humiliated so long as you include me.

It seems if people want to get down in the mouth they all have just cause. It's eye-opening to see how life in the family might look to each of our children, and to get a leg up in identifying what *might* be hurtful to them.

Certainly, we can try to respond to some of these complaints, like rallying a bit more enthusiasm when the baby learns to ride a bike, even if this is our third time through it. We can try not to overburden our eldest with responsibility for the younger siblings. And, yes, we can do more to help our middle children—who don't have as clearly a defined place—to feel more significant. We can be responsive to our children, but we must make sure in doing so that we don't show favoritism to one child over another.

CHILDREN'S PERCEPTIONS OF SIBLING FAVORITISM

There is probably nothing that hurts a child as much or as frequently as parental favoritism. We know that showing favoritism is a parenting no-no. I'll bet you already spend huge amounts of time and energy just to make sure you *don't* favor one child over the other. But here is the ugly truth: What you are doing to *prevent* favoritism is actually *fuelling* it. That's right, trying to be "fair" only makes more problems. See? Aren't you glad you're learning this stuff?

Let's look at how we respond to the following cries for fairness that backfire:

"How come *he* gets new running shoes?"

"Why do *I* have to clean it up? *I* didn't even make the mess!"

"How come *he* gets to have a friend over and *I* don't?"

"*His* pancake is bigger than *mine!*"

To really ensure everything is fair, we have to become a bean counter. How else can you tell if you've actually reached "even"? Everything now has to be judged, measured and weighed. It's bloody exhausting! Let's look at how tedious it all becomes when brothers Liam and Dakota try to figure out "fair" at bedtime:

> *Liam:* "Mom, you read two books to Dakota, but only one book to me!"
>
> *Mom:* "But you're older and the books you read have more words."
>
> *Liam:* "Yeah, but not that many!"
>
> *Mom:* "How about I read 15 minutes with him and 15 minutes with you? Would that be more fair?"
>
> *Liam:* "Okay—that seems fair."

And so the first night ends with the new "fair" arrangement. And the next night . . .

> The timer chimes: DING!
>
> *Dakota:* "Oh no, time is up. It's been 15 minutes, but we only have one page left in the story. Please let's just finish the book."
>
> *Liam:* "Mom! That's not fair I heard the timer go off. He's getting more time!"
>
> *Mom:* "Oh, good gravy!"

The micro-calculations will drive you nuts. And what about the times when "fair" is far apart? If Liam is involved in hockey and Dakota takes piano lessons, do you cut Dakota a check for $300 every time you are required to take Liam to a hockey tournament out of town to "make it fair"?

If Dakota had something like cystic fibrosis and needed hours of respiratory therapy everyday, would you try to match that one-on-one time with Liam? What would that look like if you had Liam + Dakota + two other children? No way could you keep it even.

In our quest for "fair" we end up inviting comparisons, judgment and competition between our children. Someone is going to feel they came out behind the other. That is where the quiet pain and hurt sneaks in.

I suggest we move to a different model. What if I told you we could live in families where parental time and resources are in abundance and everyone feels their needs are met at home? I will show you how it's possible. The benefit is that there will be no more feelings of one child being loved or cared for more than another, which is what you wanted in the first place. Pain goes away, revenge behaviors stop. Let's learn how.

Favoritism Solution #1: A Family without Fair

If Liam complains, "His pancake is bigger than mine," Mom could reply "I am not interested in how much Dakota has; I only want to know if you have enough pancakes for you. I have more batter, and if you would like another pancake let me know."

If Dakota complains that Liam goes to expensive hockey tournaments, Mom and Dad can say, "If you need to travel or buy equipment for your hobbies or extracurricular activities, we'll be sure to support your needs, too."

We need to send the message to our children that at various times different people in our family may need more or less of our family time, and more or less money or attention, and that is okay. We can assure our children that we are here for each other as a family, and that we'll do whatever it takes to make sure everyone's needs are met. *That* is what co-operation is all about. No bean counting for me.

Favoritism Solution #2: Don't Compare

This point I can't emphasize enough: not only am I suggesting you stop comparing pancake sizes, I am also saying we need to stop comparing our children to one another. Here are some favorite comments to throw out the window as soon as possible:

> "Cassandra was reading chapter books at your age."
> "Why can't you be more polite, like your sister?"
> "Your sister pulled off an all-A report card."
> "Your brother is really something special."
> "If he can do it, you certainly can."

These sentiments don't stimulate a child to want to do better. They pit child against child as rivals. Eventually they will become enemies. Hurt will be inevitable and, while the wounds may be invisible, this insidious psychic punishment that hurts your children's self-esteem is just as real and painful as the corporal punishment that leaves welts on flesh. Drop these lines and drop the idea of comparing kids to one another.

Favoritism Solution #3: Learn to Handle Sibling Conflict in New Ways

The next area of improvement we can work on to avoid hurting our children is to handle sibling conflict in new and improved ways. Every family with siblings has to deal with some fighting, so I've given this advice many times. I know firsthand that your initial reaction will be to balk. I have come to expect that. I also know that once I get all the information out there for you, and you experiment with the strategies, you'll change your thinking: you'll be met with success. I think you'll agree with the other parents that this is one of the most important things a parent with more than one child can learn. Yes, folks—it slices, it dices, it juliennes: Am I overselling this? We'll see...

Understanding children's roles within the family

Let's look closer at the underlying dynamics between siblings. Beside the birth order positions of eldest, middle and baby, each child also plays a role in the family. Here are some examples to give the flavor of what I mean:

The good one
The bad one
Momma's boy
The easygoing one
The sensitive one
The black sheep
The rebel
The special one
The sick one

Children choose their own roles for themselves, and then parents treat them in ways that re-enforce those roles. Kids watch each other very closely, and when they notice a sibling's weakness, they seize that as an opportunity to develop a niche strength. They think to themselves, "Hey—here is something I can do that they can't!" If Mom is urging her eldest to talk to Gramma on the phone, but he refuses or is awkward, a younger sibling might see his brother's socially conservative nature and think, "I don't mind talking and being outgoing and social. Here is a way to surpass my sibling. I'll be the chatty one!"

As soon as a child shines in that niche, the other sibling drops out to ensure there is no more competing or comparison, allowing the other to excel in it. "He is your Mr. Chatty; I am the quiet one." It's a nice little system that allows everyone to have a unique place in the family. It's actually quite co-operative.

Our eldest child does have an advantage because he or she gets to pick roles first. Eldests have free rein. However, because children are born innately wanting to co-operate, fit in and please their parents, firstborn children usually do start off life as the "good child."

Part of the reason for the firstborn good-child phenomenon can be explained by the fact that eldest children start life as "only" children. They had Mom and Dad's full attention and doting until that other bundle with booties came through the door and made havoc.

During those early years in the spotlight, the omni-presence of parents looking over their shoulder and cheering every accomplishment can result in the child developing perfectionist tendencies. After all, that feedback loop is very tight! As soon as they stack two blocks, someone immediately applauds the accomplishment. Our children want to get things right, of course. They are learning how to be a human and want to succeed. They want to color in the lines and make their picture of a flower really look like a flower.

And what better way to make sure you are getting things right than to have rules? Our firstborns love rules, and get a great sense of comfort in knowing that the puzzles go on this shelf, my coat goes on this hook, Daddy sits in that chair, and bedtime is at 7 p.m. (so let's get our jammies on). No wonder they are so responsible! They take this rule stuff all so seriously. So seriously in fact, that they can develop anxiety disorders.

The eldest tends to listen to our instructions and then do things "just so." For them, the more rules and structure, the better. Rules provide more opportunities to show you are living up to expectations and doing it right. They are every nursery school teacher's dream.

Ahh—those were the years, hey Mom? Remember that happy-go-lucky toddler gleefully doing everything you asked him to? What happened to him?

With the birth of a second child, we de-throne our good child. The arrival of a sibling means that things can go one of two ways now:

1. Either your firstborn child will hold onto her good position, in which case the new baby has to find a unique place in the family. The second child will differentiate by being whatever number one child isn't.

   That means if the eldest is the best at being good, the second child dare not try to compete in this area. I mean, look at how good she is! She asks to go to bed for Pete's sakes. So any attempt at being good is going to pale in comparison. The second child doesn't want to be the next-best at being good. He'd far rather find his own best—the best at being "bad." Do I speak the truth or what? If that is not your family's situation, then maybe option two is being played at your house.

2. The other scenario that can unfold is that our good child eldest who seems a tad perfectionist, rigid and rule-bound, winds up getting discouraged when she is faced with anything less than perfection. Hell hath no fury like a discouraged firstborn. It hurts to want to be perfect and to fail. Eldest children hate being corrected, they hate not being the first and best anymore. They may develop the mistaken belief, "If I can't be first and best, I must be worthless."

If that is the case, this once good child will start to misbehave, and, sadly, probably get punished for it. Her younger sibling, the second child, watches his older sibling acting badly and getting punished, so he learns to do all the things Mom can't seem to get his sister to do.

She won't brush her teeth. "Oh, I will, Mommy!" pipes up the second child. She refuses to say please and thank you, so the "good child" takes the opportunity to shine by developing impeccable manners. If the eldest sees that her younger sibling is better at being good, she'll let him take the role and become the "good at being bad" kid.

Maybe this should be called the Bart Simpson Complex. Of course Bart takes the "bad boy" role (although we know he is a softie) when he's up against Lisa, that vegetarian, poet, sax-playing philosopher of a younger sister. Who could come anywhere close to her?

If a third child comes along (congrats, that means you found at least 10 minutes when there weren't two kids in bed with you!), he or she will take up a role, but not good or bad if those are taken. The third child may decide to be the funny clown or the easygoing child. Most famous comedians are the third child / baby in their families. Looks like a good niche to take. Mom can't get the older two to stop fighting, so to impress her and be unique, the third child can get a one-up with Mom by being funny and easy. "No fights here, Mom!"

UNLOCKING CHILDREN FROM THEIR ROLES

Roles are not a bad thing, until people want to change and they feel they can't. How will our "bad" child ever come around if the role is glued on? We can help.

Remember Lewis our toilet clogger? He is known as the "behavior case" in his class. The teacher's beliefs about Lewis cause her to watch him more closely for incidents of misbehavior. She watches to confirm her beliefs about him. Of course, since she watches more closely, guess what? She finds her evidence. It's self-perpetuating.

Lewis gets caught for the smallest of infractions. In fact, it's not uncommon for three or four boys to all be horsing around together, but the teacher singles out only Lewis, since he is the one she watches and worries about.

As if that isn't bad enough, she punishes him harder than the other children, thinking she'll crack that nut yet—as if he is a wild horse that needs to be tamed! Lewis sees the injustice of this and it hurts. He doesn't know how to shake his reputation.

· ·

Seeing is believing—but believing is also seeing.

· ·

The same can be said for other roles. The parent who believes he has a meek and sensitive child watches more closely for evidence that he can't handle a situation. At the slightest appearance of being upset, Mom steps in and rescues the child, reinforcing his incapable role.

Here is the good news. Children are actually very quick to change. Now the bad news: we parents are not. It turns out that it's far more challenging to change a parent's attitudes and expectations about their children than it is to change the children themselves.

So here is the challenge. Can you start right now, today, this moment, to shake your preconceptions about your children and clear the baggage clouding how you think about your revenging child?

Many parents don't realize just how differently they have been responding to their "bad" child. They would if they could see themselves on video. It's overtly noticeable. I was recently on a plane, seated behind a mother and her two young boys. Whenever she talked to her younger child she corrected, scolded and generally had a terse and dismissive tone. I could see no reason for this differential treatment: both boys squirmed, but only one was told to sit still. Both were curious about the buttons and seat tables, but only one was told not to touch. Both wanted to run down the aisle when the plane landed, but only one was scolded and told that he had to wait, while the other was just tugged back to his seat.

I am sure this was due to a history of one boy being harder to handle. Yet, objectively, he was behaving no worse than his brother. Mom was indeed "picking on him" unfairly. Clearly, this mom felt justified in her tougher treatment of him. The pattern was set.

We actually prevent change when we assume the worst and maintain our patterned reactions. When we think to ourselves, "Here we go again; I am going to have to take my monster child on a plane now. I had better prepare for his antics," we fortify the problem because we will act differently in anticipation of problems.

So how do we pull away from our old patterns?

Drop the Past and Don't Assume

If you enter into interactions with preconceived notions, no doubt you will unwittingly influence the situation so that you get exactly what you expected. If you think you'll have a bad day, I bet you will! If you think you're little tot is going to spaz, you'll no doubt inadvertently behave in ways that likely participate in the factors that bring that very spaz on.

Instead, we have to remember to treat every day and every moment as if it was a clean slate. Bygones—let them go. Those other spazzes were in the past. We're creating this new moment and it can go any way we want.

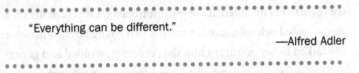

"Everything can be different."

—Alfred Adler

We only have THIS moment to influence change. Only now can we make an impact, in this very moment. Let's use that wisdom to its best potential.

Influence Positive Change by Holding Positive Expectations in the Moment

Since we have only this moment, we can use it to invite positive change in our revenging child by exuding warmth and caring, love and acceptance. They probably have not felt that from you in a while. I am guessing you're both wearing a lot of armor to protect yourselves from each other these days. Why not take some off?

We can take this moment to show we trust our children and that we expect the best from them. If they want to stand in the aisle of the plane, instead of prohibiting them because they *might* run, let them try. Leave the option for change open.

If we never let Lewis take the class attendance to the office for fear of letting him out of our sight, today is the day to give him a chance. Let's show him we expect him to do an impressive job of it. If he fails, ask him again tomorrow and tomorrow and tomorrow until he sees that we won't be fooled by his role! We are wiser. We see his goodness. Can you change your attitude about your revenging child?

Accentuate the Positive to Help Your Children Re-invent Themselves

We can help Lewis find his other qualities. Let's notice the times when Lewis is calmly standing in line and appreciate it. When he is doing his desk work, when he offers a friend a turn on the computer and the hundreds of other moments in the day that fall between his misbehaviors. Lewis does have a gentle nature in him, too. It is very powerful for our children when we seek out and notice these behaviors.

Wyatt is not *always* a slob. He is downright meticulous when it comes to his rock collection. Mom might notice that and tell Wyatt how conscientious he is with these special things. In fact, Wyatt has all kinds of strengths and qualities if Mom plays the talent scout and actively looks for them. Parents can emphasize the positive and show their children what wonderful things they bring to the family.

When we are committed to unlocking children from their roles, we help free our children to act in different ways, and avoid the stinging pain of favoritism.

SIBLING FIGHTING—TO HELP OR HINDER?

There is a difference between sibling fighting and sibling rivalry. Any two people, siblings included, have to work out their differences or learn to live with them. How parents respond to their kids' fights in part determines whether the children will resolve conflict and grow close in friendship, or become rivals.

Typically, when we see our children fighting we step in with the intention of making things better. We "break up the fight" and punish the wrong-doers. It sounds so reasonable; it's hard to believe it's misguided. However, involvement in our children's fights creates hurt and the desire for revenge: it's a painful source of discouragement for the revengeful child that I often come across in my practice.

Let me explain what's happening with our warring siblings by using a "Wild West" analogy:

Imagine for a moment that two cowboys plan to rob a bank together and share the money. The job goes sour and one of them gets caught and sent to the slammer.

The twist is this: the jailed criminal discovers that he wasn't just randomly pulled over by the sheriff for trotting his horse too quickly down Main Street—turns out, his partner actually turned him in. He goes to jail and his partner gets a Good Samaritan, award from the mayor!

Of course, the whole town gets in on it: when the convict is released from jail and enters the saloon, he gets a chilly reception, even from his favorite bartender. The Good Samaritan, however, enjoys free whiskey all over town. In fact, it seems now he can do no wrong.

One day (at high noon?) our discouraged convict meets the so-called Good Samaritan on the street. What happens? The convict is furious and wants revenge—he tosses off his coat and starts throwing punches. The Good Samaritan could fight back (and could even win if he wanted to), but since they are in public and there is a crowd watching, he decides it's far better for his saintly image to take the blows and cower passively in the attack. This makes the convict look worse, while reinforcing the Good Samaritan's innocent reputation around town. The criminal is thrown back in the slammer—this time with a longer sentence.

Welcome to the life of the "bad" child and the "good" child in your family. Hey—and you've just been deputized!

Let's see how this plays out at home, now that you know to watch for two complicit partners, where a sheriff jails one and canonizes the other.

Martin and Christa are outside playing. Every time Martin gets on his tricycle, Christa steps on the back and tries to push him faster and catch a ride. Martin wants to ride alone. His sister refuses to get off. Martin gets frustrated with her and he begins to push and get physical. She holds on. Martin finally uses his full might to tip the trike over, pitching her off onto the concrete. Mom sees this through the window and comes running out. "Martin! I saw that! What do you think you are doing? She could have hit her head on the pavement. She is just a baby; you should know better than that. You go to your room right now. I don't want you to come out until you are ready to say you are sorry to Christa. Come on Christa, we'll get some ice on that bump and you can help me bake some cookies."

Wow! Not as exciting as desperados robbing a bank together, but far closer to your reality and ultimately the same system is in play.

The theoretical points you need to know are:

1. Fighting is co-created and co-operative behavior (similar to the idea that it takes two to sustain a power struggle).
2. Our children can choose to fight or to co-operate. It is their choice.
3. Fighting (like all behaviors) serves a purpose. It is useful or effective in some way.
4. Our children get along when we are not around. They have all the skills and talents required for co-operation.
5. Our presence and reactions to their conflict is the payoff they seek.
6. Our response is to act as sheriff. We pick sides, show favoritism and reinforce the good and bad roles.
7. Even the "bad" child is content to reconfirm his belief that he is bad and treated unfairly.

Christa needs her brothers to mistreat her for her to look good and win favor with Mom. The worse he looks, the better she looks. She has no interest in finding a good solution to the trike problem. She is not looking for a ride; she is looking for a fight to prove her mother's favoritism. She knows what it takes. She relies on past patterns to repeat again, and for everyone to play their same roles.

Without Mom, Christa would make different decisions. She might see her brother getting really upset and get off his bike. She might work harder to find a solution for how to win his interest in giving her a ride. Christa is not without alternatives or skills. She actively chooses ways that sustain the conflict.

One reason I know this to be true is that they don't fight when Mom is not around. They get along famously and solve issues of taking turns and sharing with great skill when they are alone. They only decide to create a fight when the sheriff is in town.

But, what about Martin? Why does he tip her off his bike if he knows the sheriff is watching? First, he is already cast as "bad," and so he is more apt to want to revenge for past transgressions. Since he harbors the belief that every time there is a problem he is wrongly accused, he actually creates situations to confirm his hypothesis. When he is punished and she gets off, his internal belief is again confirmed: "See, I am right! I am hated and she is the loved one."

There are two goals that can be achieved when siblings fight: attention and favoritism.

Fighting for Attention

The first goal of fighting is getting undue parental attention. You've read the attention chapter already. You know on reflection that it makes sense; well-behaved siblings do get ignored, while fighting siblings hijack Dad's or Mom's time and attention every time. We can't stand it. We can't ignore it. Works like a charm!

Tory and Brandon fight whenever they are in the car together. Even confined to seat belts they kick each other and throw things across the car. Dad constantly reminds them to settle down and not fight. But it's the same every time they are in the car together.

Since this is annoying, non-escalating fighting, Dad can simply ignore it or allow a logical consequence to unfold.

"The car is not safe when you two are fighting, I'll need to pull the car over if the fighting continues." The fight continues, so Dad pulls off the road. He steps out of the car and says, "Let me know when you're ready to go again," and then he reads a book (neither looking nor listening to their fighting in the car) until the fighting stops. The kids bang on the windows: "We stopped fighting; you can drive again."

The next time a fight starts up, Dad doesn't need to state the consequence. The children know, so he simply pulls off the road, gets out of the car and reads. After five or six times, the children will no longer fight in the car. I swear this is the truth, but you have to experience it for yourself. Be consistent and do this EVERY time they fight. Periodic consequences won't work.

I recommend all parents start with this car-fighting strategy just to prove to themselves that their children can, in fact, turn their fighting on and off at will. It is a choice they make! When fighting no longer draws attention, the fighting stops. If you can master the car fighting, you are ready to move on to the other tactics I'll describe next.

Fighting for Mom or Dad's Favor

The second goal of sibling fighting is to confirm that Mom and Dad do indeed have a favorite. Curious system, isn't it?

In the trike family, it's Martin who will be doing the time, while Christa is the Good Samaritan. Later that night while Mom is watching TV, she sees Martin bop Christa over the head with his Faber light sword. Mom thinks, "See how much of a monster I am raising? That was totally unprovoked! Poor Christa was just sitting there minding her own business when he randomly attacked her. She was an innocent victim. He is such a bad boy!"

Martin is painted as the bad boy villain in his family and Christa is seen as the Goody Two-shoes who needs protection and defending. This makes Martin resentful. Since he *always* gets in trouble, he might as well hit his enemy when he gets a chance. He'll be blamed anyway, and at this point in his young life, Martin has already come to see Christa as the reason his life has become hellish. Mom and Dad prefer her. It's clear. He tests this, and it's always verified. Children like to confirm their beliefs, even those that are negative.

The lesson here is to realize that the "good child" and the "bad child" in your family work in concert to contrast their saint and sinner roles. But they are only roles. Each child has his or her own kind of weaponry and, while they may look different, they are all of matching caliber. Some use their tears to get adult assistance and some use their brain to set traps and manipulate, while others use raw power. Regardless of their tactics, kids can still decide to fight or co-operate, so no one is at a disadvantage to another. Don't be fooled into thinking someone is defenseless or incapable. The car experiment will help to prove this with your own children.

Christa could decide to stop pushing Martin's trike and to stop being a pest to her brother. She could try using her charm to get a ride. She also knows his threshold and is capable of knowing when to stop. Martin can also decide to amuse his little sister by letting her push for a bit before going back to doing his own thing. He could also negotiate some time to play with her later. Or . . . he can tip the bike. They both have choices to make. They also both have a good idea of the outcomes of their choices. They know each other, and they know if Mom and Dad are watching.

• •

"The children who need encouragement the most get it the least."
—Dr. Rudolf Dreikurs

• •

FIVE WAYS TO RESPOND TO SIBLING CONFLICT AND PREVENT HURT

Since sibling rivalry is such a huge element in the deep discouragement that can cause a child to reach for the mistaken goal of revenge, we have to learn how to handle conflict between our kids. We have to deal with sibling relations in a fundamentally different way from how most families are going about it. No more stepping in and policing their fights, arresting one and giving a Good Samaritan badge to the other. Both parties are complicit in the problems they create together, so our responses cannot single one child out. Here is how:

1. Ignore the Fighting

As I mentioned, most fighting is really about attention-seeking, which we talked about in Chapter 4. That means our first new strategy is to ignore the fighting. Let them work it out on their own and don't get involved at all. Your children will resolve things the same way they do at school or on the playground. Currently they have the idea that if they play nicely you'll leave them be, but if they fight, you'll come to police them. We can change that dynamic by letting our children know we would love to stay and play so long as people are getting along, but as soon as Martin pulls out his light saber and bonks his sister, Mom can say, "I am not interested in watching that," and leave. She can let them know she is happy to come back when they can get along.

Hmmm. That's a different reaction, isn't it? Martin didn't get in trouble. Christa's halo is not shining so brightly. Martin is not getting arrested. Change is in the air!

Christa is not likely to jump on Martin's trike and bother him anymore. He'll just push her, and that's not worth it if he doesn't get in trouble. Christa decides it's best to ask for a turn. Without Mom's interference, her old ways don't work.

Martin doesn't need to wallop his sister at random moments because she is no longer the golden child who gets him in trouble. She doesn't hang off his bike anymore, and they get along much better. Sometimes, he even wants to share his bike with her now that the animosity is gone.

2. Put Them in the Same Boat

The name of this technique says it all: put them in the same boat. Imagine it: two children in a canoe, one in the bow and the other in the stern. Both have paddles and both have different ideas of which direction they want to go.

If the two don't get along, they will go in circles. Each effort one makes to move forward is cancelled by the other. If they are in opposition, they each have the ability to stymie the other. For any progress to be made, each will eventually realize that they *must* elicit the co-operation of the other. If your boat mate is mad, he won't want to co-operate. It becomes apparent that you really do need him. By putting kids in the same boat, we stop the hurt that comes from taking sides, and we help our children learn to co-operate and love one another.

The way to accomplish this in our homes is to create in real life the metaphorical canoe experience. We put our children in the same boat by treating them as a team.

Let's say one of your kids wants to watch *Hannah Montana* and the other wants to watch *The O.C.,* they are fighting in the family room, kicking each other to get the converter. How do you put them in the same boat? You can turn the TV off, take the remote away and let them know that when they decide on what they are watching you'll give it back. They both lose the TV until they can agree.

If the children are getting more violent than you can tolerate, try this: "You both need to take some time apart and collect yourselves. You both can go to your own rooms for five minutes."

Another great line you can try: "This is a non-violent house; please take your fight outside." This shows them that you are NOT going to get involved, that you are aware that it is none of your business and it also respects that you must maintain the social order. Most often kids who receive permission to keep fighting stop right away.

If the family room is a mess, all the children need to clean it up, no matter who played with what. Does that sound "unfair"? Remember, we are not looking for the bean-counting fair; that will lead to competition. This is the abundance model where we are a team: we all pitch in, we all need one another and we all get the job done together. If you were camping, everyone would help portage *all* the gear. You wouldn't say, "I am not carrying that; it's his sleeping bag." This not only ensures no favoritism, it builds bonds for the hurting child. Now her siblings are helping her! She feels connected through the joint effort of the task.

If Christa is mad at Martin for not letting her have a turn on his trike, she can refuse to clean up the family room with him. Mom doesn't get involved in the fight. She simple restates that they have a job to do together. If Martin comes to Mom complaining, "But she won't help—she's just sitting there," Mom can answer, "I am sorry you are having problems with your sister. I am sure you can work it out with her." Mom is empathetic but she refuses to triangulate and take sides. She shows faith that they can get along if they want. The problem is Martin's to solve, not Mom's. Mom doesn't need to discipline Christa for not helping. It's none of Mom's business.

Martin is in an important pickle that we want all our children to experience. It's the problem of social living—the kind of living we are trying to promote. Martin must try to win his sister's co-operation if he wants help cleaning. He will learn that happy sisters help more, and that it's in his own best interest to be a better brother to her.

So while Christa is indeed the smaller and weaker, she is not disadvantaged in their conflicts. If we put our children in the same boat, we ensure they are equally equipped. No one is favored and no one gets hurt. Relationships improve between siblings and between Mom and Dad. The hurting stops and the acts of revenge cease.

3. Put It on the Agenda

If your children do come up against a conflict that they can't seem to solve on their own, parents can help out, but *not* by getting sucked into the fight at hand. We know now not to triangulate.

Instead, if a problem is ongoing and the children can't find a solution together, parents can offer to talk about it when people are not fired up and upset. We usually tell our children that if they can't solve it on their own, they can put it on the agenda for the family meeting and we'll work together to find a solution. This shows that we have faith that they can manage their problems, but also that we are here to support them if they feel they need it. (We'll discuss family meetings in Chapter 8.)

4. The Two-Arm Technique

Let me state for the record: a lack of skills or abilities is not the big culprit in sibling conflict. Usually, it's the sibling dynamic we just discussed. That said, there are a few skills I do recommend parents teach their children. The first is teaching our children to speak up. We teach this by using something called the "two-arm technique."

> *Carla snatches her sister's doll out of her hands and says "MINE." Her sister Dina begins to wail and look for Mommy. Well, of course she does. After all, she has learned from experience that Mom usually solves her problems for her. All Dina needs to do is sound the "tear alarm" and Mom comes investigating. Nearly every time Mom will find that the problem is Carla, and then she feels beholden to "deal" with her on Dina's behalf. It's got favoritism written all over it.*

Dina is growing up and she needs to learn to take matters into her own hands instead of relying on Mom. She needs to learn that it's her job to deal with others, especially her sister. If she continues to find success in using her tears and inabilities in order to muster help from others, to get someone else to fight her battles, she will learn that playing the victim is beneficial.

Instead, try the "two-arm technique" that I learned from Althea Poulos at Kinderschool Adlerian Nursery School. The idea is to teach children the language of dealing directly with each other when they have a conflict.

It goes like this:

When she hears Dina crying, Mom should NOT pick up Dina and console her as she usually does. That looks like she has already sided with Dina. Instead, she can get on her knees between the girls so she is eye-level with them. Gently holding one child in each arm, so they are facing each other (Mom clearly centred and not siding with one or the other), Mom can say, "Dina, do you need to speak up? Do you need to say something to your sister? She is a very good listener." (Mom has not only empowered Dina to speak, but she has also let Carla know she is not in the bad books and so she has no reason to be defensive.)

Dina doesn't know what Mom means. She sniffles, stares blankly and doesn't say anything. This is the first time Mom has asked this question. Usually Mom just gets the doll back for her and scolds Carla. What's going on?

Mom: "You need to speak up, Dina. You can say 'I don't like that.'"

If Dina still doesn't talk, Mom can say to Carla, "I think your sister is saying that she doesn't like it when you take her doll." Stated this way, Mom is just delivering a message from Dina. Compare that to: "Oh Carla, give your sister her doll back, please. You know that is her favorite thing—what is wrong with you?"

We are not policing or triangulating when we are helping Dina find her words. We act as the conduit so our personal judgment is not involved. We are staying out of it and not taking sides when we use the two-arm technique. With time, Dina will get better at speaking up, both because she has the skills, and also because the original payoff from Mom is no longer happening.

5. "Bugs" and "Wishes"

With older children you may want to use "bugs" and "wishes," which I learned from Dina Emser and Susanna Smytha, who train elementary school teachers. Again, the idea is to teach children to communicate more effectively. We can help children speak up by showing them a sentence structure using two toys as props. All you need is a stuffed bug (a ladybug works well) and a fairy wand. When your kids have a conflict, they first pick up the bug and say:

"It bugs me when you _____." (the child holds out the bug)
Then they wave their fairy wand and say:
"I wish you would _____ instead."

Dina could say to Carla: It "bugs" me when you take my doll without asking. I "wish" you would ask for a turn.

How much more informative, respectful and empowering is that statement than crying? Eventually, the children learn to use this language without involving their parents (or teachers).

ACTIVE LISTENING

I have shared the most common sources of the deep discouragement that lead to a revenge-seeking child within families. Check them out in your own family—even if today your child is only just dancing to the tune of attention. The revenge dance reveals to all of us how discouragement takes hold in our kids, and what to do to bring them back. Not only that—it can crop up in any family. There are any number of reasons a child may lash out after feeling hurt. I learned this myself the day my daughter attacked our fruit bowl.

I had just picked her up after her junior kindergarten class. We hung around the school yard for a bit, I visited with other moms and then we made our way home for lunch. Everything seemed fine until we got in the door, and my daughter jumped up on a chair in the dining room and using her thumb, she violently poked a whole in every single banana in the fruit bowl.

I was shocked! Like all of us, I had to quell the knee-jerk reaction to yell "What do you think you are doing, young lady? We don't go around wrecking things like that! You know better. Go to your room right now!" She was setting me up for the revenge dance; I knew that if I was feeling shocked and appalled then this was an act of revenge, which must mean she was feeling I had hurt her somehow. Let's walk through how to avoid this dance through active listening.

First, I checked for the source, instead of getting angry and punishing her:

"Lucy, have I done something to hurt you? Something that made you so mad at me that you wanted to get even by hurting the bananas?"

Do you know what she said? "I didn't like what you did to me at the school yard!"

I had no idea what she was talking about. "What did I do at the school yard?"

"I didn't like how you got all those other mommies together to laugh at me."

Well, my jaw nearly hit the floor. She had a totally different perception of what had happened with the moms on the playground.

I was telling them about a funny thing Lucy had done at the dinner table. I assumed she would feel like the funny comedian again if I retold it to my mom friends. Clearly I was wrong. From Lucy's perspective, at the supper table we were laughing with her, but on the school yard we were laughing *at* her. Making a silly mistake around family is one thing; having a goof publicly exposed and laughed at was quite another.

I felt terrible for my mistake and I was glad we had a chance to talk about it so I could apologize and explain that it was not my intent. I was able to see the situation from her perspective, and eventually she also saw it from mine. She understood I had not meant to shame her.

Boy, I am glad we talked.

How will we know what our children are feeling unless we ask them? And when we do, we had better be trained to listen to what they have to say.

One of the most important skills I learned during my psycho-therapy training was the art of listening. It's the keyhole through which we get into the private world of another person. If a person feels truly heard, they feel we understand them. Do you know how wonderful it is to "be gotten" by someone else? When the social masks we wear can be relaxed and we let someone into our authentic selves, it is so powerfully connecting. Now *that* is intimacy.

If you have a child who is revenging against you, you have to find out what it is that they find hurtful. My daughter Lucy told me about the public humiliation and we were quickly able to deal with the misunderstanding and make up. But not all children are so willing and verbose. Why? Because they don't feel safe to speak their minds.

In a therapist's office, a client has to be made to feel that it's a safe place to reveal themselves without judgment. If we want our children to take off the mask and reveal themselves to us, we need to understand how vulnerable they are making themselves to us, and cherish that they are willing to expose themselves this way. It is an awesome gift for someone to be open.

The better a listener you become, the more likely your children will talk to you. They'll talk about small little things, but also about important and highly personal issues. As they grow and their issues become more serious, we will be especially grateful for having established a good listening rapport with our children.

The art of good listening is the key tool for parents with revenging children, which is why it is especially emphasized here. But, please don't wait for a child to *be* revenging to use it. Start being a better listener right now and use this tool often.

Putting the *Active* in Active Listening

There is a difference between hearing and listening. Hearing occurs when sound waves hit various parts of your ear, moving hairs that stimulate nerve endings to fire signals that are sent to the brain. Unless you are deaf or wearing ear plugs (and don't laugh, many parents do), you are always hearing. You can't turn it off.

Active listening, on the other hand, involves your attention and your dedication to processing the information. You must be watching and listening to the other person with the intent of understanding them. Actively listening to our children requires us to decode the child's full message. It includes all information that is available: body language, word content, tone, speed, volume and any other information that can help you to build the full picture of what is being communicated. Then, and this step is crucial, we need to check with our child to ensure we understood what they meant. That means we have to repeat back to the child by paraphrasing or summarizing what we believe they have expressed, including information about their emotional state.

That's it in a nutshell, but it gets a bit more complicated in practice. Let's break it down into steps that can be practiced and mastered:

Pay Attention

Oh, we are all so busted! How ironic that we complain about children being "mother deaf," when they have *just* as valid a complaint of parents being "kid deaf." They're trying to tell us about their day at school and we're unloading the dishwasher, writing a grocery list and stirring the chili on the stove, all at the same time. "I'm listening, I'm listening" we lie.

Studies on listening reveal that we remember somewhere between 25 to 50 percent of what we hear.

So, if we really want to be an active listener, we need to give our undivided attention. Even if that means saying, "Honey, what you are saying is important to me and I want to hear everything you are saying. I am having trouble paying attention because dinner is almost ready and I am trying to get it on the table. Can we find a time to talk when I can pay full attention?"

Now, if your child is in distress, nothing is more affirming of their tight kerning importance in your life than to say, "Let me turn off the chili—dinner can wait. Let's find a place we can sit and talk."

It's important to not be multitasking in your mind either. If your thoughts are on something else, you won't be able to pay attention. Keep your focus on the current conversation and on what is being said. Your job is to understand. That means you need to snap yourself out of trying to build your rebuttal while the other person is talking. Just listen and try to understand.

Show You Are Listening

Your children will be more likely to continue talking if they feel they are being heard. That means you can give indicators that they have your attention and that you're taking in everything they are saying. Things like nodding, smiling, or giving a little "uh-huh." Use any facial expression that says you're following along. Check to make sure your body posture is non-defensive, that it's open and inviting. If you lean back with legs and arms crossed, you seem closed, cut off and distant. Instead, uncross your arms and legs, and lean in a bit. This is much more warm and inviting.

While eye contact is usually recommended for active listening, if relations with your child are very strained, it may be threatening. In those cases, you may wish to try lying side by side on a bed, both looking at the ceiling together, or sit on the floor back to back. You can also go for a drive while having tough conversations. These all work to help the child feel safe enough to open up.

Provide Feedback

Perhaps the hardest part of active listening is preventing our own personal biases, beliefs, filters and judgment from skewing what we hear. To ensure this has not happened, we have to repeat back what we have understood. It's helpful to start your paraphrase with, "sounds like your saying . . . " or "what I am hearing you say is. . . . " This gives the child an opportunity to correct any misunderstandings and also to feel really understood.

Here are some examples:

"I HATE my teacher!"

Response: "Sounds like you had a rough day at school. Do you want to talk about it?"

"You never like anything I do!"

Response: "What I am hearing you say is that you're angry with me, and you feel like I am critical or negative of you?"

"I don't want to go home yet!"

Response: "Sounds like you're disappointed our good time has to come to an end."

"I wish Gramma were alive."
Response: "Sounds like you're really missing her."

"Stop telling me what to do."
Response: "What I am hearing is that it really irks you when I offer my advice if you haven't asked for it."

Since you are trying to get a clear understanding, you might find it necessary to ask for more information or clarification. So you may ask, "What do you mean when you say _____?" or "Can you say more about that, I am not sure I understand."

Defer Judgment

Interrupting will only frustrate your children: they will clam up and storm off. In fact, in very stressed relationships with older children, parents can agree to just listen for a full half-hour without interrupting or replying.

This format guarantees the child can talk freely. Now, she may choose not to say anything for the first 20 of those 30 minutes (you can start with a smaller amount of time if it feels better), but she still owns that airtime, even if only to sit in silence with you staring at the ceiling or driving in silence together. It's your child's space to speak, and she decides what the time is used for. It's respectful and caring to make this time available for her. It can be frightening for children to talk about their hurts. It may take time for them to muster the courage. Be patient. The giving of your time, and your willingness to hear from them is an act of caring they'll appreciate.

Respond Respectfully

When your child has been heard, it's your turn to reply or respond to what she has said. Now it's time to test your own emotional intelligence. Can you respond honestly and respectfully, without a counterattack and without putting her down in some way, however subtly? If you practice good communication, you'll be offering your point (which is valid for you), without adding all the emotional bravado that is the stuff of war. Just make your point. For example, you can say, "I feel angry when _____," instead of actually demonstrating your anger by replying with anger in your voice.

Compare these common parenting responses that shut down communication verses active listening.

SHUT DOWN COMMUNICATION	
"I hate my brother!"	Response: "No, you don't hate him. You love him. You're just mad."
"I'm going to kill myself."	Response: "Don't talk like that."
"You always take his side!"	Response: "That is not true. Just yesterday I took your side."
"I hate you!"	Response: "Yeah, well, you're not doing much for me either these days."

ACTIVE LISTENING	
"I hate my brother!"	Response: "Sounds like you're really angry. Do you want to tell me about it?"
"I am going to kill myself."	Response: "Really? Sounds like you're feeling total desperation. I really want to understand just how how you feel about your awful life right now."
"You always take her side."	Response: "It would hurt a lot to think your parents were against you—is that what you're thinking?"
"I hate you."	Response: "You'd like me to know that I have hurt you badly, and you want me to hurt, too?"

It's imperative that you give full acknowledgement of what they are feeling in that moment. For example:

"It would be awful to feel that your parents were against you."

"It must hurt so much to think that I love the baby more."

"I can't image how painful it must be for you, feeling that my work is more important to me than you are."

Once we understand what it is like to walk a mile in the child's shoes, we can be empathetic instead of defensive. That means we can put our energy toward finding ways to make improvements. It also helps us to keep our focus on the future and on our plans for improvement. It's so easy to want to revisit the past, assign blame and rekindle old fights. Use your communication skills to stay in the moment and listen, understand, empathize and move toward the future:

"I don't want you to think those things; how can we make it better?"

"It is never my intention to make you feel that way. How can we do better in the future?"

REBUILDING THE RELATIONSHIP

How does one rebuild a relationship after it has taken a hit? It's about action! It's not enough to think, "I love you." It's not enough even to say, "I love you." We must *show* that we love our hurting child.

Love is a verb. Acting lovingly is the way to heal and rebuild. It also means working to meet our children in their world, instead of demanding they join ours. If you think your child is drifting away from the family, find out where he or she drifts to. Instead of insisting on eating a family meal (which is your idea of bonding), investigate with curiosity those things that are appealing activities to your child and get involved where you can:

- Offer to be the videographer while your son practices his skateboarding tricks.
- Take you daughter shopping at the mall. Ask her for help upgrading your make-up or hairstyle.
- Buy a collaborative video game that requires two players to problem-solve together.
- Plan a short weekend trip somewhere they might like to go: an action hero convention out of town, a dinosaur museum in another town, white-water rafting . . . the list is endless.
- Sign up for intergenerational classes: cooking, baking, karate, biking club, yoga, horseback riding. . . .
- Do a project together: fix a dirt bike, redecorate a room, build a fort, design a dress. . . .

The important part is the co-created experience. It's about being in the same bubble together. The more time you spend in that bubble, the more you will have shared experiences, shared memories, shared laughter, shared emotions, and you will find yourselves improving the bond and getting more intimate. The relationship will continue to get healthier. It doesn't have to be a big weekly or monthly time-sink. In fact, just as important and powerful are all the little things you can do each and every day, in the moment, to show you care.

Here is a list of little but powerful ways to show your kids you care:

● ●

Ways to Show Your Kids You Care and Rebuild Your Relationships

Notice them.

Smile a lot.

Acknowledge them.

Seek them out.

Ask them about themselves.

Look in their eyes when you talk to them.

Listen to them.

Play with them.

Read aloud together.

Giggle together.

Say *yes* a lot.

Tell them their feelings are okay.

Set boundaries that keep them safe.

Be honest.

Be yourself.

Listen to their stories.

Hug them.

Forget your worries sometimes and concentrate only on them.

Notice when they're acting differently.

Present options when they seek your advice.

Play outside together.

Surprise them.

Delight in their discoveries.

Share their excitement.

Send them a letter or postcard.

Follow them when they lead.

Notice when they're absent.

Call them to say hello.

Hide surprises for them to find.

Give them space when they need it.

Contribute to their collections.

Discuss their dreams and nightmares.

Laugh at their jokes.

Be relaxed.

Kneel, squat or sit so you're at their eye-level.

Answer their questions.

Tell them how terrific they are.

Create a tradition with them and keep it.

Learn what they have to teach.

Use your ears more than your mouth.

Make yourself available.

Show up at their concerts, games and events.

Find a common interest.

Hold hands during a walk.

Apologize when you've done something wrong.

Listen to their favorite music with them.

Keep the promises you make.

Wave and smile when you leave in the morning.

Display their artwork in your home.

Thank them.

Point out what you like about them.

Clip magazine pictures or articles that interest them.

Catch them doing something right.

Encourage win-win solutions.

Give them your undivided attention.

Ask for their opinion.

Have fun together.

Be curious with them.

Tell them how much you like being with them.

Let them solve most of their own problems.

Meet their friends.

Let them tell you how they feel.

Help them become an expert at something.

Be excited when you see them.

Tell them about yourself.

Let them act their age.

Encourage more; criticize less.

Be consistent.

Admit when you make a mistake.

Enjoy your time together.

Give them a special nickname.

Marvel at what they can do.

Unwind together.

Be happy.

Ask them to help you.

Support them.

Applaud their successes.

Deal with problems and conflicts when they're small.

Tell them stories in which they are the hero.

Believe in them.

Nurture them with good food.

Be flexible.

Delight in their uniqueness.

Let them make mistakes.

Notice when they grow.

Wave and honk when you drive by them.

Give them immediate feedback.

Include them in conversations.

Respect them.

Join in their adventures.

Visit their schools.

Help them learn something new.

Be understanding when they have a difficult day.

Give them good choices.

Respect the choices they make.

Be silly together.

Hang out together.

Make time.

Inspire their creativity.

Accept them as they are.

Become their advocate.

Appreciate their personality.

Talk openly with them.

Trust them.

Share a secret.

Write a chalk message to them on the sidewalk.

Create a safe, open environment.

Be available.

Cheer their accomplishments.

Encourage them to help others.

Tackle new tasks together.

Believe what they say.

Help them take a stand and stand with them.

Daydream with them.

Do what they like to do.

Make decisions together.
Magnify their magnificence.
Build something together.
Encourage them to think big.
Celebrate their firsts and lasts, such as the first day of school.
Go places together.
Welcome their suggestions.
Be sincere.
Introduce them to new experiences.
Share a meal together.
Talk directly together.
Be spontaneous.
Expect their best; don't expect perfection.
Empower them to be themselves.
Love them, no matter what.

Source: The International youth and childcare Network

Now, surely there are things on that list you can get cracking on right away. Start small, but aim big. Be patient. And remember: never give up on your relationship with your children.

Speaking of giving up, we'll move along now to our next chapter which looks at how to parent the child whose mistaken goal is assumed inadequacy. These children are masterful at making us want to give up on them. But we're going to learn how not to. Ready to tackle the last of the four misbehavior dances? Even if your child does not do the assumed inadequacy dance with you, I am going to share *the most critical parenting concept,* and it applies to all families, all children and all forms of misbehavior. It is the "universal tool" for every parenting situation, so read on.

CHAPTER SEVEN

ASSUMED INADEQUACY

Please Hear What I Am Not Saying
by Charles Finn

Don't be fooled by me
Don't be fooled by this mask I wear
For I wear a mask. I wear a thousand masks
Masks that I am afraid to take off
And none of them are me
Pretending is an art that is second nature with me
Don't be fooled
I give you the impression that I am secure
That the water's calm and I am in command
And that I need no one
But please, don't believe me, please
My surface may seem smooth, but my surface is my mask
Beneath lies no smugness, no complacency
Beneath dwells the real me in confusion, in fear and in aloneness.

I panic at the thought of my weakness and fear being exposed
That is why I frantically create a mask to hide behind
To shield me from the glance that knows
But such a glance is precisely my salvation. And I know it.
That is, if it's followed by acceptance.
If it's followed by love
It's the only thing that can liberate me from myself
From my own self-built prison walls
It is the only thing that will assure me of what
I cannot assure myself,
That I am really worth something
But I don't tell you this, I don't dare
I am afraid to
I'm afraid that your glance will not be followed by
acceptance and love.
I'm afraid that deep down I am nothing
That I am no good
Only you can call me into aliveness
Each time you are kind and gentle and encouraging
Each time you try to understand because you really care
With your sensitivity and sympathy
And your power of understanding
You can breathe life into me
Please try to beat down these walls
with firm but gentle hands
Who am I, you may wonder
I am someone you know very well . . .

Reprinted in an abbreviated form by permission of Charles Finn. For the complete version see www.poetrybycharlescfinn.com.

No child is going to do a better job of convincing you that you have "wrecked them" than the child whose goal is assumed inadequacy. These children are the most discouraged of the lot. They have been trying tirelessly to find their sense of belonging and importance and, sadly, they have failed repeatedly.

Why is that? What happens in the life of our children that they can't find their way to love and acceptance, to significance and belonging? They want it from us, and we want to give it to them. How come we don't line up? Crazy, isn't it?

Every parent needs to learn the critical information in this chapter because it will help solve that impasse, and get our children back on the path to good mental health.

Whether you're dealing with attention, power, revenge or assumed inadequacy, the one major antidote for all discouragement is the same: encouragement. It's time to figure out what encouragement is all about—how we can give it, where we mess up and how to get better at it.

• •

Misbehavior is the symptom.
Discouragement is the disease.
Encouragement is the cure.

—Betty Lou Bettner

• •

So you see, I have left the best for last! There is no more profound skill than to learn to be an encouraging person. People are naturally drawn to encouragers. They have a certain aura about them. You enjoy being in their company because you feel you are the best version of yourself when they are around. On closer inspection, you realize that the "best" version of you is your authentic self, allowed to be fully expressed. Being an encouraging parent is a gift (and indeed medicine) you can give your children. It's also a skill to develop and a mindset to possess.

Unfortunately, typical child-rearing practices being what they are, our children are faced with years of discouraging experiences. In the case of children who have the goal of assumed inadequacy, their track record of discouraging experiences is longer and they feel their discouragement more deeply. They start to abandon hope that there is any way left for them to belong and feel significant.

These children develop a deep fear that they may really be worthless and unlovable. This belief doesn't happen over night, or from one bad day. For these children, it's the end of a long journey of trying. It's human nature to toil in order to overcome some feelings of inferiority, but when we lose all hope of ever overcoming them, we give up. That is why I urge every parent to read this chapter. If your child has not yet hit this deep level of discouragement, this chapter will teach you how to prevent it.

UNDERSTANDING THE CHILD WITH THE GOAL OF ASSUMED INADEQUACY

The dance of assumed inadequacy is concerned with the child's goal to protect themselves. They do a good job of it too. After all, drastic times call for drastic measures. I can understand their choice of tactics. I mean, if you were close to bankrupt, what better security than to hoard your last few dollars in a secret place?

These kids are like a turtle that has pulled its head back into its shell. They avoid being judged poorly by staying out of the judge's circle. It's a brilliant method of coping really, but maladaptive. We want our children to engage in life without the fear of failure constraining their efforts. We want to inspire them to grow and be all they can be.

At least, we wanted that for them at one time. The brilliance of this dance is that parents become discouraged as well. Now Mom and Dad have come to believe they can't help their children. They lose hope of improving their children. Finally, parents throw their hands in the air and say, "We give up," convinced they have tried every conceivable thing to get their children out of this foxhole they have dug for themselves.

Duping Mom and Dad is the child's creative solution to get away from pressure to "try, try, try" to be better than they are. When Mom and Dad finally throw their hands in their air and say, "We give up—we've done everything, there is no hope for this child," the child has actually achieved what they set out to do.

"HALLLELUIJAH!" says the child with the goal of assumed inadequacy. "Finally, some relief from the pressure to be *better* and to be *more*. I've managed to disappoint them for so long and so consistently that they have finally given up on me and hopefully now they will just let me be. My little scheme is working! I don't want to try. I don't want to even be noticed. Leave me alone."

That is the payoff. "I will act with an air of inadequacy that is so convincing, you will stop trying to make me 'better.'"

Along with the proper diagnostic steps set out in Chapter 3, you will notice these children have a different feel about them. While attention kids are more like pesky flies and power kids come out with two fists swinging, living with children whose goal is assumed inadequacy is like living with Eeyore. They can be slow and slouchy, showing no ambition, which usually means another sibling or the parents do. They often slack off or fail at school, which usually means there is already a high-achieving scholar in the family, and they are more likely to be layabouts. These are likeable people that everyone else wants to "fix." They either avoid activities all together, or else they start a project and then quickly abandon it. In fact, they don't like new initiatives at all. Let's see if we can find out more about why this is so, by gaining a better understanding of "courage."

BORN WITH COURAGE

No child is born discouraged. In fact, quite the opposite. Babies are born with what we call "native courage." This is the courage to stand naked and exposed to our fellow man, to show others our whole being. With native courage, we reveal our true selves to others even though we are flawed, humble and imperfect beings. It's the courage to be imperfect and the courage to try. Even in the face of potential failure we are willing to reveal our inadequacies publicly. Now *that's* courage!

If you can handle that, my friend, you have got the very best of life. It's mighty wonderful to be able to stand boldly and say to the world, "Here I am. And right now, as flawed as I am, I am okay just the way I am." Now that's a healthy self-esteem.

• •

"Imagine what you could do if you knew you could not fail."
—Unattributed

• •

Every new life is wired to follow a path of maturing, developing, unfolding and evolving across the life cycle. At any given time, we are "less" than the completed version of ourselves that we are working towards. So every person at each moment is an "imperfect" version of their completed self. See, we do just keep getting better!

I guess our most perfect day is the day we die, because then we are as complete as we will ever be.

The baby wants to become the adult, just as sure as a tadpole wants to progress towards a frog, a caterpillar towards a butterfly. We don't need to spur them on or given them stickers or money to motivate them. Nonsense. It's natural. Our kids want to become adults and join society as a full-fledged, contributing member.

And tadpoles, caterpillars and babies all feel just fine about the struggle to get there. A tadpole doesn't feel like a failed frog. A baby who is struggling to learn to walk and talk doesn't feel she is inferior. Babies blissfully go about learning. They aren't humiliated when they say "ba ba ba," even if everyone else is saying "supercalifragilisticexpialidocious."

But along the way something changes. Our children begin formulating mental constructs about themselves, others, the world and how it all operates together. Parents set the stage and our children get swept up in it. We create the illusion or paint a fiction that there is a scale of worth and that you can rise up or fall down depending on what you do and how you "perform."

THE SLIPPERY POLE OF SUPERIORITY

Most of us operate as if this pole really existed, the pole that says people at the top are worth more than people at the bottom. But the pole is slippery. We have to grip it desperately and try constantly to crawl up. It's hard work!

But even after we hit the top of the pole and reach our destination of being supposedly "superior" to others, we're never sure we can keep our grasp. The higher we raise ourselves up the illusionary pole, the further we fear we may plummet. The pole itself creates anxiety.

The superiority pole creates a sense of transience that leaves people deeply unsettled, as if it could all be fleeting; as if we are only as good as the last good thing we did. We can't ever relax and just be. It sucks up all our energies that could be better used getting on with life and growing. We're so consumed with not losing our position on the pole that we become very cautious and fearful of anything that would jeopardize our position. Do any of the below describe you?

- Have you ever shied away from hosting a dinner party, fearing it might be a flop? Think of all the friends and fun you've missed because you're fearful your cooking isn't up to par, or your house is not pretty enough to entertain.

- Do you avoid trying a new hairstyle because you're fearful it might look bad? How horrid can a bad cut be? Will you die? Hair grows back. Have fun with your renewable resource. Since when did bad hair make you a lesser person?

- Have you passed up a job opportunity thinking, "I'll never get that." Have you ever flubbed at something, then made the proclamation, "I am never doing THAT again!"

- Think of your children now. If your son tries a math problem and can't get it right away, does he crumple the paper and give up? If you try to teach your children a new skill, do they say "forget it," if they can't immediately get the hang of it?

Well, someone needs to tell the Emperor his bits and tackle are flying in the wind: there is no pole. You are safe! We don't need to prove our worth. It was never in question. We don't have to earn it, and we never have to fear losing it. We need not worry about a "failure" that could knock us downwards. A failure means only that we made a mistake we can learn from. It can't take away from the valuable human that you are.

How wonderful does that feel? To know that right now, as you are, in this moment, you are all that you have to be. Once you can believe that, you are free to tackle life fearlessly.

So which mindset or narrative do you want your children to learn? What will you teach them? We can parent in ways that will create "pole climbers" who are preoccupied with their ego and how they compare to others. Or we can raise "path walkers." We can choose to pave a path and guide our children down a road that has no ego concerns. This is the encouragement path that is dedicated to helping our children grow and develop so they can fully self-actualize.

CHOOSE TO RAISE A "PATH WALKER"

We can choose to adopt a different narrative. We can raise our children in a family that does not buy into the pole of superiority fiction. Instead we can be guided by a more meaningful and constructive narrative about people and their life journey. We can refuse to believe and participate in the habit of evaluating people's worth and merit based on judging their performance. We can agree that all humans are born in complete wonder, and that they don't have to prove or perform in order to earn acceptance or love. We can reject the notion of "good, better and best" people. If we don't, we're creating conditions that will see the rise of another Hitler. Who dares decide who is "better" than others?

Following this new path leads to mastery, not superiority. This path embraces human differences rather than imposing judgment. Sure, an A in math is better than a B, but that simply indicates that right now you know more about math, not that you are a better person.

This approach knows that you are able to develop yourself, and that the more mistakes you can bear to make, the more you are trying new things and living life at your growing edge! This path also appreciates the gifts and talents of each person and pays attention to those strengths.

Children raised in a family that operates under the belief that life is concerned with upward striving can easily become discouraged. Their internal world gets shaped and arranged very differently from the encouraged child.

WAYS WE SHUT KIDS DOWN AND HOW TO DEVELOP THEIR COURAGE INSTEAD

There are so many subtle ways that we accidentally discourage or "shut down" our kids in our day-to-day dealings with them. Unless it's pointed out, most of us would never realize it. Of course, once I make you aware of it, you'll find examples everywhere, and you'll realize just how prevalent this issue is for children.

Parents often tell me after learning about the encouragement and discouragement process that it almost pains them to overhear the conversations between most adults and children. Let's look at a few common scenarios together so you catch my drift. I am sure there are a few scenarios here you'll recognize from your own personal repertoire. Don't beat yourself up if you discover you've been shutting your kids down. Before this book, you didn't know—now you do. That's all. Remember, mistakes are opportunities to learn. No ego worries anymore, okay? You're not a "bad parent." If any of the following scenes were stolen from your living room, it is because you were operating with less knowledge, and now you have more information. You're in a position now to make a conscious choice to adjust your parenting approach and benefit from what you've learned. It should feel exciting. (This was an example of being encouraging by building on strengths and minimizing mistakes. It feels good, doesn't it?)

Build Confidence in Your Child's Competency and Skills

Children are born with few skills and competencies; they must develop them. Their lack of skill can be a source of their inferiority feelings, so it's best if we work to encourage them to overcome these inabilities and become competent. We can either inspire them in the process, or we can emphasize their deficiencies.

For instance, say Jamie wants to pour his own milk and Mom says, "No, Jamie, that's Mommy's job. You'll spill it." Jamie's mom has just given him a vote of non-confidence. What she is really saying is, "I don't believe in your abilities," and she has snubbed his natural desire to take initiative.

How many similar comments have you heard along the same vein that emphasize children's inferiorities? Let's look at some examples, followed by an alternative comment that provides encouragement:

"You're too little to use a knife." (*Would you like to try using a butter knife? After some practice with that, I'll show you how to use a sharp knife carefully.*)

"That slide is for big kids; come use this little one." (*I can see how careful you are being, crawling way up that big slide!*)

"No skateboarding, you'll kill yourself." (*You can try the skateboard if you're interested, but you must be wearing the proper safety equipment.*)

"I know you like hockey, but I wouldn't be dreaming of the NHL, buddy." (*"I am so excited that you have found something you are passionate about—go for it!"*)

"That's breakable; let your big brother put the ornament on the tree." (*"This ornament is made of glass and is breakable. Can you show me how you use your careful hands with this one?"*)

Develop Confidence in Your Child's Judgment

Besides physical competencies and skills, our children need to develop their cognitive abilities and sense of judgment. This is also part of moving from undeveloped to developed, from being a neophyte to approaching mastery. Children flex their judgment muscle *if* they get a chance to exercise it and learn from their mistakes. We prohibit growth if we overstep them and undermine their abilities to make judgments for themselves. Here are some examples, followed by alternative comments that show confidence in the child's judgment:

"Put your sweater on; it's chilly." (*"I am wearing my sweater today. It's too chilly out there for me, but I trust you to decide that for yourself."*)

"Two more bits of stew before you get down from the table. . ." (*"I am sure you know your tummy best and can tell for yourself when to stop."*)

"That's not enough of a gift for a best friend; get him something else." (*"Looks like you have chosen exactly what you'd like to give as a gift."*)

Notice Efforts and Improvements

The only way that children can approach mastery is to make an effort and work through a series of sequential improvements. Rarely does anyone embark on something new and do it perfectly the first time. If we want to encourage our children to "stick with it" and continue to develop, we have to be *encouraging of the process*. That means we must focus on the value of making an effort, and recognize improvement as the goal. If we only value perfection, our children will feel discouraged every time they come up short. For instance:

"Oh look, you made your bed; let Mommy fix those wrinkles for you." (*"Wow, I can see you worked really hard on that!"*)

"You call this clean?" (*"You sure take pride in your bedroom. I see you've got everything picked up off the floor and all your clothes put away."*)

"Ninety-seven out of 100? What happened to the last three marks?" (*"Your hard work is paying off."*)

Take a Positive Attitude about Making Mistakes

Mistakes are a necessary part of the learning process. Embrace mistakes as opportunities to learn, and you encourage growth and persistence that will lead to mastery. If we ostracize children for mistakes, those mistakes will be perceived as failures and children will begin to lose courage. They will restrict their experiences and stop trying anything that may yield a mistake. Consider these scenarios:

"Oh, now, look at the mess you've made." You've got pancake batter all over the countertops." (*"You made pancakes! I can't wait to try one. Cleaning up is a part of cooking and baking, so let me show you which type of cloths we use for these types of spills."*)

"That's not right; let me look after it." (*"Looks like you're working on a plan. Keep at it; you'll figure it out."*)

"Now you've ruined it." (*"I guess that didn't work the way you expected, but I am sure you can work around it somehow."*)

"You had the wrong dates—if you'd just stop and think for a change." (*"Oh, I have had that happen to me! What a merry mix-up life can be sometimes. Oh well. We'll live."*)

Develop Your Children's Abilities to Handle Themselves and Life Situations

When we are young, the bumps in the road of life are small. As we have more and more experiences of getting over little hurdles successfully, we gain skill and belief in ourselves to be able to face progressively larger moguls. Encouraged children have faith they can manage. However, if we intervene and rescue our children from facing their own personal struggles, we stunt this development and discourage them into believing they can't manage. Consider these different approaches:

"I think you should have gotten a higher mark; I am going to talk to your teacher about this." (*"It sounds like you have a legitimate concern about the marking. You should bring it up with your teacher and see what she has to say."*)

"My daughter is shy; she doesn't like to talk to strangers. She wants the grilled cheese and French fries." (*"It's your job to speak for yourself. I am sure you will do just fine. When you are interested enough, I am sure you'll muster up the courage to do it."*)

"That boy has been nothing but a problem to you. I think you should end the friendship and move on." (*"I am here if you*

want to talk about it, but I am convinced you can straighten
this fight out with your friend.")

"Your father is clueless; let me talk to him." (*"I can understand*
how you must be feeling. I am happy to listen and offer a hug,
but I am convinced that you can handle this matter with your
dad directly.")

When we change the messages we send our children, it alters their
beliefs about themselves. These encouraging messages are rich with
the positive Crucial C's and help counter those feelings of being
disconnected, incapable, discounted and without courage.

Now some readers might be thinking to themselves, "Who would
ever talk to their children so negatively? Didn't they learn anything
about self-esteem building and being positive?" These days, many
parents have decided that ensuring their child is cheerful all the time
will result in them being encouraged children.

WRONG.

Here are the three pitfalls that cheery parents need to keep an
eye out for.

Protecting from "Bad" Emotions

Please don't think that by delivering the disappointing news that
"this is the last game of Candy Land before bed," you are somehow
discouraging your child. Expect children to be upset or disappointed about having to face some of the demands of life. There
are limits and boundaries that must be enforced and respected.
Bummer. You are not being discouraging. In fact, quite the opposite.
By showing them they can manage to live within limits, children
learn they *can* manage. When we bend the rules for our kids, we
are being discouraging because the deeper message is that we don't
think they can handle it. Don't feel a child must always be gleeful

to be encouraged. Don't feel it's your job to cajole your children into happiness at all times. Just be supportive as your children face perceived hardship.

Encouraging Our Children While Berating Ourself or Others

Sure, you would never be harsh on Timmy if he accidently made the mistake of grabbing the unopened end of the bag, thereby scattering chocolate chips in a million directions. Sure, chocolate is poison to a dog, and Mollie the golden retriever is lapping up as many as she can while you chase her with the broom. But don't worry, Timmy; it was an accident. Let's get it cleaned up together and try again.

But what if *you* accidently upended the bag? What if *you* burnt the cookies you both worked on? If you forgot to stop and pick up the dry cleaning? Are you just as gentle on yourself as you are on Timmy? Or do you take a strip off your own side? "I can't believe I did that. Where is my head today? I am so mad at myself! GRRRR..."

You can bet that Timmy is taking in those messages, too. What do you think he makes of that? "Gee, Mom *does* like perfection and Mom *does* judge people. Boy, she sure *doesn't* forgive her little mistakes!" The message received might become, "If she doesn't like her own mistakes, then she probably doesn't much care for mine either. She was covering up."

You can see that we have to be more global in the messages we send to our children. That means to be encouraging as a person, you have to embody the idea wholeheartedly and live your own life with this belief. So ask yourself: are mistakes okay? How many have you made today? I recommend you make a good five or 10 mistakes a day. That means you're living on the edge of your growth curve too. Otherwise, you're playing it safe. GROW! It's exhilarating.

Confusing Encouragement with Praise

Ever since the University of California at Berkeley days of "Everyone's a winner and everyone gets a trophy!" we've been loading on the compliments to our children in an attempt to create good self-esteem. We have to make sure they feel good about themselves, right? So let's really tell them so, and heck, let's even stack the deck so they get the winning hand with praise:

> "Good girl."
> "You're the best."
> "You got an A!"
> "You did that just perfectly!"
> "You always know how to please me."

Aren't these positive statements, too? There's no discouragement here, right? Most parents say these types of things all the time, but believe it or not, these are in fact discouraging statements. Popular literature and Mommy magazines use the terms *encouragement* and *praise* interchangeably, but they are vastly different. Praise is just a verbal reward. Rewards are used to lure and manipulate children into behaviors. The reward is not given until the adult deems the child has hit some imposed standard. Then, Jackpot! Here is your little (verbal) sticker.

Praise is chock full of appraisal and judgment; it's just that the judgment is favorable. When we use praise, we are promoting the idea of "pole climbing" that we talked about earlier. In essence, we communicate that our children are on the pole, but, hey, they're at the top!

For many of us who were raised on praise, we think it's the *best* thing to give to a child since we yearned for it ourselves. We're projecting and regurgitating the tapes in our head. Well, of course that makes sense if you think about it. One of the issues I have with praise is that since it's dependent on external judgment, you don't develop your own self-appraisal systems. How do you know if you are doing okay unless some authority deems you "okay"? "How was my lasagna; was that okay?" "What do you think of this new hair style. Do I look okay?" "Am I a good parent? Do you really think so?" To be validated becomes a critical mission for the person raised on praise, and most of us were! Of course, we assume it's just what our sons and daughters want to hear, too. But all we are doing is passing the baton of self-doubt to the next generation.

Since praise involves judgment, there is always the fear that we could lose our parent's approval at anytime. When an A on a report card is celebrated, a child frets about the potential B that might be coming home on the next report card. In fact, the child might even opt for less challenging classes, in order to keep those As coming. Dave might decide that he will sign up for the basketball unit in gym since he knows he is good at that. He is really interested in the archery class, but who knows how that will turn out? Sadly, the praised child declines the option of growth.

Am I suggesting you don't celebrate an A or cheer success? No. But praise, like stickers, is only given to completed work that meets specific, goal-oriented criteria. It misses entirely the process—it misses what takes place on the path towards mastery. I have brought home many good grades that I did little work to achieve. However, the mark I am most proud of was a 52 percent in first-year university calculus. I had not taken high school calculus and I was totally lost. I got 17 percent on the first midterm, but I needed the math credits for my science program or I was going to have to change faculties. I worked like I had never worked before in my life, and I passed.

It is NOT the final mark, that simplistic A, that matters. It is the effort and the improvement that counts. Who cares what others think of my work? It is how I feel about my scholastic accomplishments that matters.

So sure, you can be interested and happy for me. Go ahead and ask, "Hey, you got your marks: how do you feel about them?" And you can even say, "You sound really proud, congrats! Let's go out to dinner and celebrate the end of term."

If you had a glowing-star sibling, the one who had sun shining out of her butt, you know that living around praise is incredibly discouraging.

Hanna (age four) and her sister Clara (age seven) are both drawing pictures at the table. Clara starts drawing a picture of a horse, and Hanna, who looks up to her big sister, decides to draw a horse too. Hanna is upset because, try as she may, her picture really looks more dog-esque, and she can't seem to make the image in her head come out the way she wants on paper. Her sister's picture is clearly "better." Mom comes by and says "Oh, that is a great picture, Clara—and so is yours, Hanna." Mom is such a liar! Hanna is not blind. One is better—obviously.

In a world that values perfection, Mom's false praise is noticed. Let's face it, with a three-year handicap, Hanna will spend a great deal of time being "behind" her older sister in the skills she is developing. But since praise is only given for final completed perfect work, Clara will receive more praise than her sister.

However, anyone and everyone can be the recipient of encouragement. Anyone can put in an effort. Everyone can improve. Encouragement emphasizes the process rather than the final product so that all ages, all abilities and all qualities are valued. Giving your best is what is important and honored. "Being the best" is not.

Instead of Mom being the art critic and lying to placate Hanna, she could have sat with Hanna and said, "I like your drawing. You've been working hard on it. I noticed all the attention to details you put in too. Do you want to tell me about it?" Mom is giving encouragement because she is noticing Hanna's efforts rather than focusing on the outcome or the "picture quality" that is (or isn't) accomplished.

This is a critical shift in our focus when working with children who have the goal of assumed inadequacy, because they feel they will never hit the top. Deeply discouraged children feel that they have slid way down to the bottom of the slippery pole of superiority. They are choked by their feelings of inferiority. The idea of ever reaching the top of that fictive pole is so overwhelming and, frankly, unbelievable, they don't even bother trying.

Such children need to know that *any attempt* is worthy, just for the merit of trying. The discouraged child needs to see that little baby steps are the way to success. They need to be shown successes in small increments to rejuvenate their motivations and to believe in themselves again.

Common Parenting Pitfall: Over-Hyping Initial Progress

Of course, if your discouraged child has not made any effort in ages, and he or she finally musters the courage to take that first baby step, the worst thing a parent can do is throw a ticker-tape parade. "Oh my *goodness*! Look, our picky eater tried a bit of cantaloupe! Oh my, look who decided to clean her room! I am going to take a picture and text it to Dad at work. He'll flip! You're going to try out for the school musical—I AM SO PROUD OF YOU!"

Your child will think, "Yikes! Retreat! Everyone is looking again."

The best approach is to create an environment that allows your children to practice building their courage in a low-threat atmosphere. We need to offer encouragement without pressure and without giving up. Let them know you have faith in them should they decide to try something new. Let them enjoy their own success for themselves. It's their "win," not yours. Suspend all judgment while holding fast to an attitude of complete faith and unconditional acceptance.

> *Josh can't seem to get the hang of skating. He spends more time down on the ice than up on his blades. His dad is the coach of his team and Josh knows that it's really important to Dad that he learns to skate. Josh wants to quit. He hates falling down in front of an arena of bystanders, publicly revealing his inadequacies.*
>
> *If Dad says, "Come on, keep trying, you'll get it, keep working on it," he is encouraging effort and stick-to-itiveness, but it's coming off as "performance pressure." Josh knows his dad is a skater and that he wants a son who is a skater. He knows, therefore, that he is disappointing his dad.*

Dad could be more encouraging if he gave Josh permission to be his own person and if he reinforced the idea that it's okay if Josh is not interested in skating. Dad loves him just the same. Josh's interest has to lead the way, and then Dad can inspire with words of encouragement. It may be that practicing skating on a flooded rink in the back yard when everyone is just goofing around is a less threatening environment than an arena with a formal "lesson."

Encouragement is as much an art as a science. Try to get inside your children's private world and make some guesses about what might be the source of discouragement from *their* perspective. What could be stirring up those feelings of inadequacy?

Here is a great, quick resource that clearly delineates the difference between praise and encouragement.

The Difference between Praise and Encouragement

	PRAISE	ENCOURAGEMENT
Dictionary Definition	to express favorable judgment of; to glorify, especially by attribution of perfection; an expression of approval	to inspire with courage; to spur on: stimulate
Addresses	The doer: "good girl"	The deed: "good job"
Recognizes	Only complete, perfect products: "You did it right."	Effort and Improvement: "You gave it your best," or "How do you feel about what you learned?"
Attitude	Patronizing / Manipulative: "I like the way Suzie is sitting at the table."	Respectful, Appreciative: "Who can show me how we should be sitting right now?"
"I" Message	Judgmental: "I like the way you are sitting."	Self-Disclosing: "I appreciate your co-operation."
Used Most Often with	Children: "You are such a good little girl."	Adults: "Thanks for helping."

(continued)

Examples	"I am proud of you for getting an A in Math." (Robs the person of ownership of achievement)	"That A reflects your hard work." (Recognizes ownership and responsibility for achievement)
Invites	People to change for others	People to change for themselves
Locus of Control	External: "What do others think?"	Internal: "What do I think?"
Teaches	What to think; evaluation by others	How to think; self-evaluation
Goal	Conformity: "You did it right."	Understanding: "What do you think/feel/ learn?"
Effect on Self-Esteem	Feel worthwhile only when others approve	Feel worthwhile without the approval of others
Long-Range Effect	Dependence on others	Self-confidence, self-reliance

Adapted from Jane Nelson and Lynn Tott's Teaching Parenting Manual (a part of the Positive Discipline Series)

HOW WE CAN ENCOURAGE OUR CHILDREN

The whole idea with encouragement is to improve our children's confidence in themselves. We have to get the idea across that they are good enough as is, and not just as they "might be." If you are psyched to be a master encourager, here are the tools of the trade.

1. **Avoid discouragement.**

   You'll never fill up a bucket that has a hole in it. It only makes sense to begin the encouragement process by eliminating discouragement. Punishment and praise are the enemy. Take down the sticker charts and burn the naughty mats. Put those sibs in the same boat so there is no more comparing or favoring. Inferiority feelings be gone!

2. **Work for improvement, not perfection.**

   This is a new way of thinking. How can we give accolades to the child who forgets her homework at school three days in a row? Well, by my calculations, that means she did remember two days this week and that is one time more than last week. THAT is an improvement. That is what we are rooting for! Let go of the "end goal" and set your sight on the next little goal.

   I took up running in middle age. The first day, I couldn't run to the end of my block. But month by month I added a bit more distance. I am going to run my first half marathon this year. If I started out thinking I was training for a half marathon, that first day would have been so overwhelming that I would have stopped. But instead, I took up running just to be active and healthy and to see what little bit more I could manage. That attitude took me the distance, and it can with your child too.

3. **Commend effort.**

   It's all about effort. Do our children know that their effort is more significant than their results? Mostly we save our comments for judgment day and then dole out praise for what they have accomplished. I want to flip that around and put the accent on a different syllable—let's focus our noticing and our comments on their labor instead of the fruits of their labor. "You were really working hard there!" If we can generate effort, success is guaranteed to result eventually.

4. **Separate the deed from the doer.**

   We have to convince our children that we love them just the way they are. However, if we say "You're mean," "You're lazy," or "You're bad," the child assumes these are fixed traits, that it is who they are. She thinks, "I am mean." "I am lazy." "I am bad."

Instead we have to emphasize that behaviors are chosen, and *that* means we can make different choices. Children are not trapped; they are free to change. Our job is to convey the message "No, you are not mean, but you are acting meanly. You could choose to act nicely instead." Said this way, we reject the behavior without rejecting the child.

5. **Build on strengths, not weaknesses.**

   Every child has talents and strengths as well as weaknesses and shortcomings. It's a far better strategy to highlight and activate our children's strengths than to dwell on their faults and foibles. Every child has what it takes to get along just fine in life, if we let them utilize their talents!

6. **Show your trust.**

   Of course, that means you have to trust your children. Do you? Trust must come first.

7. **Don't view mistakes as failures.**

   We need to take away the stigma of failure. Failure usually indicates a lack of skill. One's worth is not dependent on success.

8. **Failure and defeat will only stimulate special effort when there remains the hope of eventual success.**

   Ambitious parents may notice that when they have a failure or defeat, it usually tends to motivate them to work harder and to win next time. However, a sense of failure won't stimulate a deeply discouraged child who has lost all hope of succeeding.

9. **Stimulate and lead, but don't push.**

   We must resign ourselves to the reality that our children must move at their own speed. Sometimes that feels painstakingly slow, but it's still the better tactic in the long run. The high school dropout who decides to complete Grade 12 in middle age might have finished earlier if she hadn't felt her parent's pressure to do better in Grade 10. However, when children decide they want to accomplish something, they do! Let's stop putting up discouragement road blocks.

10. **Remember, genuine happiness comes from self-sufficiency.**

    Children need to learn to take care of themselves. Have you taken time for training (TTFT)? Are you willing to back away and let your children manage their lives *their* way? Stop infantilizing and let your children astound you!

11. **Integrate children into the group rather than treating them as "special."**

    Treating children as "special" is a death sentence. It only serves to increase their over-ambition. An over-ambitious child who cannot succeed will usually switch to the useless side of life with the private logic: If I can't be the best, I'll at least be the worst. Even more seriously, she may give up altogether. Feelings of security come with "fitting in" and being integrated into the family, not with being elevated above others.

12. **Don't stimulate competition—it usually does not encourage.**

    Those children who see a hope of winning may put forth an extra effort, but the stress is on winning rather than on contribution and co-operation. The less competitive your child is, the better able they are to stand competition. Stop saying things like, "Let's have a race to see who gets dressed the fastest."

13. **Remember that praise is not the same as encouragement.**
Praise may have a stimulating effect on some children, but praise often discourages and causes anxiety and fear. Some children will come to depend on praise and will perform only for recognition in ever-increasing amounts. Success accompanied by praise reserved only for results may make the child fear, "I can never do it again."

14. **Help develop the courage to be imperfect.**
We all need to learn to take mistakes in stride and learn from them—children and parents alike.

15. **Remember that success is a by-product of effort.**
Being preoccupied with the obligation to succeed is intimidating. The resulting fear and anxiety is often the very thing that winds up interfering with our children's performance and it contributes to failure.

Instead, we should emphasize to our children that it is their willingness to be useful and to contribute that is important, and that success is often the result of that co-operation.

16. **Don't give responsibility and significance only to those who are already responsible.**
The "good children" just get "gooder" because we give them all the responsibilities and significance. Instead, let's make opportunities for discouraged children to take on some significance and responsibility so that they might decide that it is worthwhile to offer up some co-operation.

17. **Remember: discouragement is contagious.**

    Be cautious that you don't become discouraged yourself! Have faith, take baby steps and remember that mistakes are okay. Build on effort and improvement. You'll get there.

18. **Avoid trying to mend your own threatened ego by discouraging others or looking down on them.**

    Check yourself. Have you been raised on the slippery pole of worth, and do you find that it helps you to feel "one up" in your own ego protection to knock your child down a peg?

19. **Overcome your pessimism.**

    I know; this is easier said than done, but attitude is powerful. You have the ability to choose to take a fresher outlook on life. You can develop an optimistic approach to life!

The Special Language of Encouragement

You probably have already noticed that encouragement has its own language, and since it is not the lines we heard growing up, we need our own lexicon. Following are some examples to get you going. Notice that the emphasis is on children's abilities and efforts to manage and take ownership of their work. The parent acts almost like a mirror, reflecting back what the children should feel proud of for themselves. These comments all underplay perfection and instead show our children that our own personal values put effort above the value of perfection. These are supportive comments without being judgmental.

Phrases that Demonstrate Acceptance

"I like the way you handled that."

"You did a great job tackling that problem."

"I'm glad you enjoy learning."

"I am glad you are pleased with it."

"Since you are not satisfied, what do you think you can do so that you will be pleased with it?"

"It looks as if you enjoyed that."

"How do you feel about it?"

Phrases that Show Confidence

"Knowing you, I'm sure you'll do fine."

"You'll make it."

"I have confidence in your judgment."

"That's a rough one, but I am sure you'll work it out."

"You'll figure it out."

Phrases that Focus on Contributions, Assets and Appreciation

"Thanks, that helped a lot."

"It was thoughtful of you to_____."

"Thanks, I really appreciate_____, because it makes my job easier."

"I need your help on_____."

To a family group: "I really enjoyed today. Thanks."

"You have skill in _____.Would you do that for the family?"

Phrases that Recognize Improvement

"It looks as if you really worked hard on that."

"It looks as if you spent a lot of time thinking that through."

"I see that you're moving along."

"Look at the progress you've made." (Be specific; tell how.)

"You're improving in _____." (Be specific.)

"You may not feel that you've reached your goal, but look at how far you've come!"

Encouragement is the universal salve for the human soul. Don't limit your new skills to your children. Practice on yourself, with your partner, your co-workers, your parents. If we accept the truism that *all* people want to "do good" and the only pre-requisite is for them to "feel good," we are off to the races.

Kids will understand this concept, too. I was buying groceries the other day with my daughter, and the sales clerk was very abrupt and rude. Instead of taking it personally, my daughter said afterward, "I guess she must be discouraged."

As our discouraged children find their crucial C of being courageous, they feel safe to come out of their shell and once again engage in life. It's exciting to see children who have been shut down show a renewed willingness to try, to reach out and show a desire to be co-operative. With each new step, and each successful hurdle they overcome, they rebuild their belief in themselves. Their attitude becomes more optimistic, and the spiral down turns into the spiral upward. Encouragement is amazing.

In the next and last chapter, we'll bring it all together with the final tool you'll need to run a democratic home. I'll teach you about family meetings. Even if your children are pre-verbal, you'll want to know how to get these meetings started. The meeting is the backbone on which all the other tools hang, so don't miss this key element.

CHAPTER EIGHT
FAMILY MEETINGS

I have been chomping at the bit, wanting to teach you the most important tool for your new parenting toolbox: the Family Meeting! We've spent these last chapters diagnosing our children's mistaken goals and helping them find their Crucial C's through positive means. Well, family meetings really are the cure-all. What can I say? They work.

If you're reshaping your family to the democratic ideal, one that is ruled "by the people, for the people," then it only makes sense to have "town hall meetings."

These meetings are the backbone of a democratic family. It's the venue where the whole family comes together to decide on matters that affect family life. It's important team-building and it's social equality in action. Your children will see very clearly that a big change is afoot. The structure of the meeting ensures each child is truly heard and represented. We can really show them just how much they do count, and how much of an impact they have on shaping family life.

The family meeting is where we build our social agreements together, and it's the process of co-creating them more than the rules themselves that is so vitally important to the family getting along. Why? Regardless of how brilliant the rules are, they are only as strong as the willingness of people to abide by them. It's the goodwill created at the meetings while hammering out the arrangements of living together that will largely determine whether or not our children feel inclined to follow the arrangements. The more they feel a sense of belonging in the family, have input and share ownership for the decisions, the more likely they are to live with the decisions made.

All 4 C's are nurtured at the family meeting; It's a veritable smorgasbord of mental health. Children who grow up with family meetings learn to be effective communicators and adept problem-solvers, and we all know those life skills will serve them well outside the family.

I grew up having weekly family meetings. I can tell you firsthand, these were not always Norman Rockwell moments with children acting as little parliamentarians. Sometimes they looked more like something you'd see on *Jerry Springer*. However, they kept us tight as a family, and even all these years later we still feel the impact of them. In fact, my brothers and I recently had a family meeting to discuss the sharing of our summer cottage. It works just as well with grown-up siblings as it did in our childhood. Everyone knows the drill.

But back as kids growing up in a busy house with working parents, I have images of my three brothers and me gathering around the dining room table on Sunday evenings. One brother lying on the floor, ten feet from the action (listening, but not willing to take a seat with the rest of us). Another brother threatening to use the "talking stick" as a weapon, and me, the baby of the family, acting as secretary and thrilled to have such an important task. I loved that I could always count on the weekly meeting to feel heard and to be taken seriously.

Yes, there were some tough meetings, but they weren't the norm. They cropped up from time to time between the more placid ones. Good or bad, family meetings were just what we did. And the same has carried through to my own family. Even when my daughters are planning on having friends to the cottage for the weekend, I call a meeting and include the company. They appreciate being involved and shaping the events that are about to unfold. We need to create a food menu for the weekend together, and we discuss chores and possible activities that involve me (tubing, waterskiing, trips to the marina for penny candy). In fact, the very last time we made plans to take their girlfriends to the cottage, they all agreed to help me paint the front porch! The meeting set a beautiful tone for the entire weekend.

I have old family meeting minute notes (and audio tapes) from my childhood that I love looking at. I also periodically record our family meetings for my children's memories. And you know what? The same stuff comes up in my family's meeting as when I was a kid—and the families I coach report the same. Let's face it, every family has to figure out for themselves things like:

What to do with those extra dishes that don't fit in the dishwasher when it's your turn to load. Are they now considered to-be-washed-by-hand dishes and so they are still your job? Does the *next* person on dish duty load them up into the dishwasher? Or are you expected to unload your load and then re-load partially before your duty is over? What the heck!

These are the kinds of logistical problems every family faces, but there are also deeper issues such as talking respectfully to one another, not invading others' privacy, asking to borrow things before you take them and then promptly returning them. . . . Are any of these sounding familiar? These make the issue of moldy lunch boxes left in knapsacks seem like a cinch to solve.

If all you needed were answers to these problems, I'd cough up a book called *Just Answers*. But you know why that won't work—imposed solutions never take hold successfully. Empowerment and improvement come from solving problems together as a family. When you do, something magical happens between you. Over time and across problems, people begin to feel cared for. They like seeing issues get resolved and knowing they were part of the solution. The conflict declines and the harmony increases.

Okay. I don't want to over-sell it, because it does take work. There are new parenting skills for you to develop, and new skills your children will need to learn for the meetings to be fruitful. You can even tell them that. They love seeing their parents humbly stumble along. Let them know, "I have never had a family meeting either—let's learn how to do this together!" How democratic is that?

Mostly, I want to stress to you that family meetings (and indeed the family fun that follows) are a foundation for your parenting practice, not just some cute little "add-on" for the administratively anal crowd. Just because family meetings are the subject of the last chapter doesn't mean it's an endnote. Family meetings are the culmination and the crescendo of all you've been learning.

Let me walk you through the structure of the family meeting, the basic how-to and the nuts and bolts. Then we will look at stages for gradual implementation because it's a boat load to ingest all at once. We'll end with some ways to really leverage the meetings to reach out to your discouraged children.

WHEN TO BEGIN?

As soon as your eldest child can say, "I don't want to go to bed!" or "You're a dum-dum," it's time to start your family meetings.

You're initial family meetings will look a whole lot different from the ones you'll be holding when your children are 10, 12 or 15, but by starting early you get the groundwork laid, and all the skills taught while their enthusiasm is high, and family conflict is low.

"Do we really need a chairperson, a secretary and a talking stick to discuss how the caps should back go on the marker so they don't dry out?" Yes! Later, it will be second nature to talk to your teens about returning the car clean and with the gas replaced after they borrow it.

I'll be suggesting a few stages of family meetings. If your children are very young, you may decide to stay with Stage One family meetings for a longer period of time before moving to Stage Two. Use your own judgment, and add complexity and skills to the mix as you see fit. Every family starts at a different place and proceeds at a different pace. Trust yourself to know when the family is ready to kick it up a notch.

Include the littlest members of the family in the meeting by setting them up in a high chair, and giving them a snack or a few quiet activities to do. I know, I know—why bother, right? Because it does make a difference. It's a gathering of the family, and as a family of social equals, no person is discounted because of their age. Also, who knows when your youngest will first decide to chime in at the meeting? Children understand language long before they can speak it.

FREQUENCY OF MEETINGS

Meetings need to be a weekly event. Put your family meeting on the calendar, make it a reoccurring task on your Outlook, or set a reminder on your cell phone, whatever works for you. Honor it as you would any other important appointment—the kind of appointment where they charge you if you don't show!

Meetings are held weekly to keep the feedback coming, and so the ideas and decisions stay fresh and vibrant. If you have just decided on a way to improve the system for delegating dish duty, you want to have fast feedback on whether it was an improvement or if the idea tanked. Also, and this is key, children are willing to live with even agreements that they don't like or that are not working if they know they can re-evaluate them in a week's time. If you get lazy and patchy with your meetings, co-operation will start to dwindle.

LENGTH OF MEETINGS

Short and sweet is the best way to go. But, the length of the meeting, and when you meet could actually be the first thing you decide as a family. Don't feel pressured to come up with the perfect meeting time; you simply need to take a good stab at something for everyone to try, and then see how it goes, knowing you can tweak it. Aim for about 15 or 20 minutes as a starting point. You can get a lot done in 20 minutes. Here is what one mom shared:

> Thought I'd share about our back-to-school family meeting . . .
> hadn't had one for a long time, and it was a really nice way to
> reconnect. There are four kids in our family who are in grades
> 7, 6, 1, and a toddler. We recently decided we didn't need a
> nanny anymore, so we had lots to talk about! We talked about
> housework, of course, and everyone agreed that we didn't
> want to spend money on a cleaner as we're trying to save up
> for Disney. I volunteered to do the housework for the next
> two weeks until the kids are used to their new school routine,
> and we agreed to divide the chores more evenly at the next
> meeting. We also discussed mornings, bedtime routines, who
> will be making the lunches (the kids), and someone suggested

and did type up a lunch menu for every day of the week, so I would know what to buy ahead of time. I asked if anyone would be willing to bring their younger sister to/from school as I need to get to work in the morning, and in the afternoon, the toddler naps. We talked about house keys and where they would keep them. We also quickly went over our extracurricular activity schedule and revised it a bit. . . . Lastly, we talked about the guinea pigs, sigh . . . that's another post! I'm with you, Alyson, about keeping it nice and short; it probably lasted 20 minutes.

CHAIRPERSON

Yep, we need someone to take the leadership role and keep everyone on track. Initially, this can be Mom or Dad since they probably have some experience chairing meetings from their work or service clubs. Then, and this is really important, the children should be trained to chair the meetings as well. Each child can co-chair alongside a parent until they have it figured out, and each can then lead meetings independently. This should be a rotating job. My eldest chaired her first meeting at the age of five. Children really do a wonderful job, and the sooner we are able to hand over the reins to our children, the better. The chairperson leads the family through each of the agenda items. They help to maintain focus and keep the meeting flowing forward. A poorly run meeting with no agenda or time-keeping is a death sentence. The chairperson calls on people to speak, recaps what is being said, walks people through the problem-solving steps that I'll soon be teaching you and checks in with the group to see if consensus has been achieved. The chairperson also lets the secretary know of any final decisions to ensure they are recorded.

SECRETARY

Being the secretary is a job for anyone old enough to write. The secretary doesn't need to scribe the entire meeting verbatim, just log the decisions made, and make a note of any follow-up items that might be forgotten if they were not recorded. Buy a journal to keep your meeting notes bound together for future nostalgic memories. If any confusion arises during the week about any agreements made, the meeting minutes can be reviewed. "Hey, Mom, didn't you say you'd take me shopping for winter boots after work on Thursday?" "Nope. Check the journal; I believe we said Friday."

ATTENDANCE

The family meeting is a voluntary town hall. While people do not have to attend, they do have to live by the decisions made by those who did participate. If you have a reluctant child, let her know that you really think she has some keen ideas that the rest of the family could benefit from, and that you hope she'll come help the others. With a warm welcome mat extended each week, and a true desire to get your child's valued input, she will eventually decide to check you all out. Of course, I don't need to tell you that if you start a power struggle over attending, your child will never join in. Don't go there. Instead, have lively vibrant meetings and trust that your child will eventually want to join in the action.

BUILDING CONSENSUS

Ah yes, the elusive consensus. Most people assume that means you're going to get all your children to think the same way and love the same ideas. Not bloody likely. That is why we use the phrase, "build a consensus." When consensus doesn't come easily, the chairperson must use his skills. Part of the chair's job is to move the group towards one idea, and get everyone to agree to *support* the idea (not necessarily to love it).

• •

Participating in Consensus

"I have had my opportunity to sway the group to my way of thinking. Having failed that, I will go along with the group in order to help us all move forward."

• •

Well, that certainly is community-minded and co-operative, isn't it? The person who agrees to support the group is giving a gift to the group and should be recognized for that by all. One for the team—thank you! This way, the person who was the dissenter feels appreciated and sees that he or she is helpful. If you don't adopt this system of consensus building, you'll have the dissenters always being outvoted by the majority. That creates a divide in the family.

THE AGENDA

There should be an agenda for every meeting. A suggested format is listed here:

Schafer Family Meeting: October 3rd

1. Appreciations/encouragement
2. Follow-up on old business
   a. Socks in the family room—Mom
3. New business
   a. Can I have a Halloween party? —Zoe
   b. Troubles finding fast things to pack for our school lunches—Lucy

4. Planning / scheduling / syncing calendars
5. Distribute allowances
6. Weekly chore sign-up
7. Closing / fun

1. Appreciations / Encouragement

We spend so much time finding fault in this life; rarely do we stop to focus on all that is going well. Guess what? There *are* a lot of great things going on in your family. Starting the meeting with appreciations sets a positive tone and reminds us we are gathered in the interests of getting better as a family—not to get people in trouble.

How this step happens varies widely from family to family, but so long as it's positive, you're headed in the right direction. In our family, I ask: "What made this a good week? What things happened in the Schafer family this week that make you proud of how we are doing as a family?" Some families take turns centering one person and giving them encouragement, letting them know what things they did this week that others were grateful for. Don't be put off if in the beginning your children are tight-lipped. There may be some deep animosity and also suspicion of these new "meetings," so they may not feel generous about sharing their thoughts and feelings. Some children don't know what it means to give an appreciation, but if you take the lead and show them by example, each week this part of the meeting will get richer and more meaningful. In fact, this is the *most* important part of the meeting. If ever you can't hold the family meeting for some reason, at least do this part.

2. Follow-Up on Old Business

The secretary will need to flip back to the previous meeting notes and share what was to be implemented during the week. Then the whole family evaluates how the solution is working. Does the solution stand for another week, or does it need to be tweaked? Do we need to go back to the drawing board? It is so freeing to know that we are just working at the next iteration of a solution, rather than feeling that we were wrong, or botched it. This also means that no one feels it's a prison sentence when they agree to an idea. It's a short-lived commitment. No pressure.

3. New Business

Somewhere central in the house, like the door of the fridge, there should be an agenda for the family meeting posted so that during the week, as things come up in the moment, people can jot down their name and add their items.

If Evan is having a meltdown because he desperately wants the Scoobie Doo costume at the grocery store, you can say, "I see you really would like to go as Scoobie Doo for Halloween this year. Can I put Halloween costumes on the agenda for you to discuss at the family meeting?" That is often enough to stop the tantrum. At the family meeting, Mom can also offer to sew a costume, or take him to the costume store where they may have a better Scoobie Doo offering. If Evan feels that the family meeting is where good things happen and where people really do try to make things work in your best interest, he will not mind passing up the first exciting Halloween costume he sees.

Common Parenting Pitfall: Acting Open-Minded When You're Not

Mom has no interest in buying that cheaply made over-priced costume. She tells Evan they'll talk about it at the family meeting, but in reality she has already made up her mind. She is holding off on delivering the bad news. If Mom comes to the meeting with her mind made up, and is not interested in solving problems, but in pushing her own idea, the spirit of the democratic meeting process is lost. Can you come with an open mind? Model that to your children.

Show them how people can learn and integrate new information in a way that is not "wishy-washy."

It is during "new business" discussions that the chairperson will have to lead the discussion most closely. We will look at conflict resolution and getting to consensus in more detail in just moment.

4. Planning, Scheduling and Syncing Calendars

Between the poster board you're fourth grader needs for her school presentation on the solar system, the knee pads her sister needs for the volleyball tournament, the orthodontist appointment for her brother and, yes, didn't you say you would help with the cookie dough fundraiser?—they meet at school tomorrow. HELP!—you forgot the car had to go in for service today.

Not everyone is a "planner" (including me). Having a standing item that relates to some kind of planning will help the family be proactive instead of reactive. You'll be surprised how many fights can be prevented, just by discussing in advance any upcoming events. You'll also be amazed by how little your children know about what is going on in *your* life. It's a lot harder to hear that Daddy can't make it to your ballet recital as you're getting your hair put in a bun for the performance than to have seen it marked on the calendar since last week.

Your children will see you have a life and your own commitments too! Go figure. It's a good reality check. All too often we just pull our children from place to place, and they have no sense of control over their comings and goings. It's more respectful and democratic to co-ordinate everyone's time.

5. Distributing Allowances

Since the family meeting is about managing the business of family life, it seems a good fit to use these meetings as a time to pay out allowances. I want to be clear on my position. Every child gets an allowance, regardless of whether or not he or she attends the meeting. Allowance is not a reward for attendance. Most parents tell me they forget to give their children their allowance and then get so in arrears they can't even remember what they owe their child anymore. Imagine if your paycheck was handed out this erratically! If we want our children to act responsibly and keep their commitments to us, we had better do the same to them.

6. Weekly Chore Sign-Up

Do not give allowance based on doing chores. We give our children money just as we give them clothes and shelter. It's needed for living. And, similarly, chores are a requirement of family living. But that doesn't mean the two are related or tied together. If you start that, you'll be bean counting again in no time. Don't do it!

Instill the idea that we all need to pitch in to make the family operate smoothly. We don't do it for money; we do it because it is needed.

By divvying up chores, our children participate and contribute in ways that make them feel even more a part of the family. Chores are a positive source of C's.

The family meeting is a good time to address the work of the family that needs to be done in the week ahead, and to delegate these responsibilities among the family members. It works best to let the children come up with some system. The more input they have in how chores should be handled in your home, the more likely they are to do them.

7. Closing / Fun

After your meeting, have some fun together as a family. That's right—fun!

You're all assembled anyway, and if the meeting is short and sweet, you might still have some popcorn left over. Why not put away the agenda and play a game of Crazy Eights or grab some scrap paper and play a game of charades or Pictionary?

It doesn't have to be anything big: just a nice ritual. Closing fun helps everyone stay inspired about the meetings, and it helps to end on a feel-good note, especially if anyone was feeling a little put out that their suggestion didn't get accepted.

I promise this will be the day of the week your children come to love the most. Forget all the other enrichment activities you pay big bucks to enroll your kids in. *This* is what our children desire the most from us and their family—camaraderie in work and play.

MEETING STAGES

If you try to incorporate every detail of a family meeting at once, it's likely to be a pretty spectacular failure. There is a lot to learn for everyone and doing that learning in stages will make for a smooth transition.

Stage One: Setting Expectations

The first step is to set positive expectations about what these new-fangled "family meetings" are. In some families, the kids will be excited right away. In other families, it takes an attitude adjustment. Many families have tried family meetings before, so re-introducing them may bring on moans of resistance. I'm guessing the old meetings were a flop because they were not really democratic. All too often, family meetings are just the authorities cracking down on the underlings with stronger laws. Who'd want to re-start that tradition?

The aim of Stage One is to begin the meetings on the right foot. They begin as short, fun, happy times where children dominate the conversation and parents mostly listen (that will shock and excite them). Stage One also helps the family to become accustomed to the regularity and punctuality of the meeting.

Stage One has only two agenda items: appreciations and planning for "family fun" this week. That's it. No chores, no solving fights—just a positive family meeting to solve the problem of "what to do for fun." Who doesn't want to solve that problem? Everyone is interested in having some say in shaping a fun event. It's a problem-solving task that can't go too far wrong, and it gives us the opportunity to teach a few basic meeting skills:

1. Taking turns talking
2. Solving a problem
3. Reaching consensus
4. Chairing a meeting

Of course, when our children *finally* get to speak up and be heard, watch out! They usually fight to have the floor and talk over one another. It just goes to show what a scarcity good listening is. Initially, your kids will be thinking, "Quick, I have the floor, Mom and Dad are listening—better blurt it all out and talk over my twerp of a little brother. My ideas are way better than his."

Expect this in the beginning. It doesn't mean your children are rude and need to be talked to about manners. They simply have to be taught the skills of taking turns and listening to others. That is why these early meetings are stripped down to the basics, so we can focus on building skills.

We want to set the expectation that family meetings are a time both for listening to others as well as being heard. We can prove to our kids that they don't need to worry about competing for air-time. In fact, at family meetings, there is an abundance of time and attention for EVERYONE to be fully heard.

A fantastic tool for this comes from the Native North American Indian tradition of using a talking stick. Whoever has the stick is free to speak without interruption. The other members remain silent.

You can use almost anything for the talking stick, but consider decorating it together as a family, maybe even borrowing from the following traditional, metaphorical adornments:

- An eagle feather tied to the talking stick gives the courage and wisdom to speak truthfully and wisely.
- Rabbit fur on the end of the stick reminds us that our words must come from our heart and so they must be soft and warm.
- A blue stone reminds us that the Great Spirit hears the message of our heart as well as the words we speak.
- A shell, iridescent and ever changing, reminds us that all creation changes; days, seasons and years all change, and people and situations change, too.
- Four colors of beads—yellow for the sunrise (east), red for the sunset (west), white for the snow (north) and green for the earth (south) —are symbolic of the powers of the universe we have in our hands at the moment to speak what is in our heart.
- Buffalo hair (or a reasonable facsimile!) gives the power and strength of this great animal to the words of the speaker.

Kids eat that stuff up, and parents can also learn from the wisdom of the tribal council. Practice passing the stick during the appreciation part of the meeting, going around the table one person at a time. The chairperson may have to keep order by saying, "Thank you, Emily. We are interested in what you have to say, but it's Jeffrey's turn at the moment; he has the talking stick." With practice, your kids will discover that it is okay to wait their turn, both because it *is* coming, and also because it's nice to have everyone pay attention and listen seriously once your turn arrives.

Next, the chairperson can ask, "What are we going to do for family fun this week?" It seems like a simple question, but au contraire! What day will you have family fun? What time? What will you do? Do you have a budget or any other constraints? The talking stick may be passed across the circle again, allowing anyone who doesn't have a comment to pass.

Since different people will have different ideas about what to do, we have our first problem or conflict to solve.

BED Model for Solving Conflict

We want to put our troubles to "BED" so we can use that short form to remind us of the three steps of problem-solving:

  Brainstorm solutions
  Evaluate
  Decide on a course of action

Brainstorm Solutions

We want to feel free to toss ideas out there without any fear of them being judged as "good" or "bad." This is the creative part of problem-solving, and the more wild and free you are, the better solutions you'll get. It's hard to be creative (engaging the right brain) if the rational side (left brain) is simultaneously trying to evaluate. Also, our children who are fearful of mistakes and still shakey about their feelings of courage will not want to toss ideas out there if they fear we will judge their ideas as poor. We have to deem this a criticism-free zone.

The secretary should write down all the ideas that come from the brainstorm. Parents can offer ideas, especially if children need some help getting the ball rolling, but I recommend you toss out ideas that exemplify a range of options, rather than providing the answer that is the most likely to be chosen. We are trying to show we don't have all the power. We want to model making mistakes and being creative.

What should we do for family fun? Mom says. "How about learning to crochet together? Or collecting moon rocks?" The secretary writes those down. Even if it's a lousy improbable idea (crochet together?), remember, no evaluation at this point and there is also no concern for whose idea it is. Just offer them up and write them down. This adds a feeling of anonymity that also helps people feel more courageous about sharing their ideas.

Evaluate

Once you have a list of possible ideas compiled, then you can start the process of evaluating them. You'll need to eliminate items based on some criteria, for example, "We only have so many hours," or "so many dollars," and so on. Essentially, you are creating a short list of things the kids are most keen on, and that are doable.

Decide on a Course of Action

The chairperson will need to guide people to build consensus. Remember, the form of consensus we are trying to achieve addresses the reality only for this *one* week, and we can move forward only with *one* idea. We need everyone to get behind one idea, even if it's not each individual's favorite idea. Start with a show of hands to see if you are getting close to consensus. The chairperson can say, "Looks like there is a lot of interest in going swimming as our family activity. Peter, is that something you would be willing to go along with to help the group?" If Peter says yes, we can thank him for his gift to help the family. What—sounds too Brady Bunch? You doubt your children will give so freely of these "supposed" gifts of consensus? I'll tackle how we deal with deadlock in a moment.

Once you get through the BED steps, there are usually some details and delegations to be worked out. Since we are always trying to team build, we can find ways to give people responsibilities for contributing to the family fun.

- Who will call to find out the pool hours?
- Who would be willing to load the car?
- Who can look after getting together towels for the group?

If everyone volunteers to do a little something to make the outing work, it truly feels like a family team working harmoniously towards a common goal. That swim will no doubt be fun, and fight-free. The closer-knit the family, the more likely even more co-operation will ensue at each subsequent meeting, since bridges are being built and bonds are growing richer.

At the next family meeting, people can share how they liked their time at swimming, and part of the appreciations can be about how everyone did their jobs to help the family.

Stage Two: Adding New Business: Tackling Bigger Problems

After you've established positive expectations for family meetings and practiced the skills of problem-solving and reaching consensus on non-contentious issues, you are ready to tackle bigger issues.

Stage Two involves adding new elements to the meeting, including problem-solving issues your children need help with—NOT a problem you are having with your kids. We are still showing children that these meetings are about them having a voice in the family and pushing power away from the parental control they have come to expect.

These new business items might include things such as: Jack wants a pet goldfish; Trina wants to switch bedrooms with Melanie; Paul wants to sign up for karate lessons; and Jack wants to talk about getting more time on the computer for his games.

The same problem-solving steps and skills are used to solve these types of problems, so your Stage One practice will really pay off now.

Don't fret if you don't want Jack to have a pet goldfish. Remember, it's by consensus and you have a say too! However, just saying *no* is not advisable. Instead, share your concerns and rationale for why you think it's not a good idea. Let others try to resolve those concerns.

If Jack pays for the bowl, fish and fish food, and if he is prepared for what might be the short life span of a goldfish, what other concerns do you have? You can clearly state that while you won't "interfere" with Jack getting a fish, you are unwilling to feed his fish or remind him to feed his fish.

Stage Three: Solving Those Intense Family Problems

By now, your family should be feeling like a much more tightly connected team. You've been having a lot of family fun and also experiencing the empowerment of joint problem-solving. You're ready for the bigger issues. These issues are the ones most likely to polarize: sibling fighting, talking in respectful tones, curfews, homework and so on. Also, parents can now add some of their burning issues to the agenda as well.

The chairperson will have to be assertive in enforcing the use of the talking stick, and will have to work to keep people from rehashing or rekindling their fights at the meeting.

The past is not relevant. We don't care about past transgressions. The chairperson need to focus on identifying and "naming" the problem that the group is being asked to solve. That can be a tough task. Consider this scenario:

"I never get any help with cleaning the kitchen; we're supposed to work on it together, but Trisha is always on the computer trying to sneak onto her Facebook account—that Mom said she is NOT allowed to have—before Mom comes home and catches her."

"Well, I would help if you weren't such a slacker yourself!"

The chairperson replies, "So, the problem we have to solve is what to do when you're supposed to be working together and the other person is unwilling to help or do their share?"

The chairperson works to restate the problem without naming names, taking the issue outside of the personal realm. Notice that tattling didn't work?

If the fight continues and the girls add, "You never let me on the computer after school, so when do you think I'm supposed to be on it, loser?" the chairperson can keep order by pointing out, "It sounds like sharing computer time is another problem we need to address. We can write that down as a separate item, but for now let's stick with the one issue we already have on the go."

I think you can see why it helps to build up to these types of meetings.

In the example above, the girls brainstormed solutions and they decided that for a week they would try doing their chores not as a team, but alone on alternating days. When the meeting came around the following week, and they reviewed old business, both girls shared that they didn't like working alone. Having experienced the alternative, both were motivated to work together, and the fighting stopped.

WHAT INTERFERES WITH MEETINGS?

The family meeting can be a hotbed for misbehavior. The whole family is gathered with Mom and Dad's full attention; it's a good place to enact the dysfunctional dynamics in the family. If we are wise to this phenomenon, we can actually use the family meeting as a therapeutic tool to bring about change.

Once family meetings are fully up and running, we actually have two separate goals, as parents, that we must keep in our mind. One is to discuss where we want to go for family fun, and if a goldfish is a good idea, etc., but the second goal is to deal with the interactions between people that sabotage the family; we need to find those "teachable moments" in the meeting. Expect meetings to sometimes go "badly," and remember that the most emotionally charged meetings are full of teachable moments.

. . . .

"If there are any ills that democracy is suffering from today, they can only be cured by more democracy."
—New York Governor Al Smith (1923)

. . . .

USING THE FAMILY MEETING TO BENEFIT THE ATTENTION-SEEKING CHILD

What do you expect your little attention-seeker to do at the family meeting? Squirm in his chair, be the family filibuster, act silly . . . if we are wise to this, we can use the family meeting to provide positive attention.

We can ask him to do important jobs, like preparing the popcorn for the meeting, calling people together when the time comes to start the meeting, and pouring and serving drinks.

Not surprisingly, your attention-seeker may require a longer turn on the talking stick. That's okay, so long as he's not filibustering. You can ask him for his thoughts more frequently, and thank him for his great contributions and ideas. You can also show appreciation for his patience while allowing others to speak and for being an attentive listener.

You might invite him to sit beside you and make extra efforts to touch his leg or rub his shoulder. If he fidgets, disrupts and distracts, let him know that he looks bored and restless, and remind him that he is free to go if he doesn't enjoy the meeting. It's not mandatory to stay. However, if he does stay, you'd like him to remember others' right to have our full attention.

These are all important ways to fulfill your attention-seeker's need for connection (without feeding his negative attention-seeking) that will simultaneously encourage him to participate in the meetings, which now make him feel so good.

USING THE FAMILY MEETING TO BENEFIT THE POWER-SEEKING CHILD

Power kids are going to be the most suspicious of these new "family meetings." They will be concerned with whether or not the meeting is a new way try to control or overpower them. They want to know what you are plotting! Since they are bent on proving you can't make them, or are determined to show you they will do what they want, expect them to initially challenge you at every turn. Expecting this will help you to cope when it occurs instead of berating yourself for not having a smooth meeting.

"Ah," you think to yourself. "Here is my power child, testing me and the system. I am excited about the chance to prove to her that I am NOT trying to overtake her." This is a moment to show her otherwise; it's a chance to challenge her beliefs. Don't flee from this moment because it's stressful. Consider these situations:

1. Benny is called to the family meeting and says, "I don't want to come."

   Mom says, "No? Really? That's your choice, but you have so many good ideas. We could really use you there, but it's your choice to make."

2. Lily is at the family meeting and it's time to give appreciations. She has the talking stick but won't talk.

   Mom says, "It's okay if you don't have anything to share at the moment, you can just pass the stick along. You don't HAVE to share."

3. The family is working on solving the problem of the morning routines and getting people to school on time. James is certain his parents are talking about him "in code" and that they are trying to manipulate him into being punctual. He is not participating in the discussion. He's slumped in the chair with his arms crossed over his chest.

   Mom asks, "Is there anything we can be doing to make things go better for you, James?

   He says, "No." He's sure that anything he says will be used against him.

   "Okay, sounds like you've got a plan for yourself. Let us know if we can help in anyway."

James is shocked that the meeting wasn't about getting him to do something differently. A few minutes later, James loosens up and joins in the conversation.

I'll bet that Benny, Lily and James would all be great chairs of a meeting, too. It's a positive expression of power to be called on to act as leader. I would work to involve them in this role as soon as possible.

USING THE FAMILY MEETING TO BENEFIT THE REVENGE-SEEKING CHILD

The child who feels hurt might want to ruin your meeting. The trick is not to stop having meetings. Just accept that you may have some challenges in getting them up and running. Most often, revenge-seekers will set a trap that involves proving the family is against them by refusing to help reach consensus. Here's an example:

The Parkers are just starting family meetings and are trying to solve the problem of what to do for family fun on the weekend. All the siblings want to go to the wave pool. Everyone, that is, except Collin. He wants to play paint ball. No one else likes paint ball.

Collin is expecting his family to overrule him and force him to go swimming. In fact, his refusal to go swimming is part of his method. He sets the situation up to prove, once again, that the family doesn't care about him and his ideas. He wants to reinforce his idea that he is the marginalized one in the family—the outsider no one cares about. With majority rule, he would be discounted. But we are committed to consensus.

Mom and Dad recognize his discouragement and his oppositional stance for what it is. "Collin is an important member of this family, and he is not interested in going to the wave pool; we need to find an idea that everyone likes. I am not interested in doing something that Collin doesn't agree with. Let's look for other suggestions since I know we can find something that everyone will get behind," says Dad.

If further brainstorming doesn't generate anything that Collin is willing to agree to, then the chair of the meeting can say, "We are nearing the end of our 20 minutes. It doesn't look like we've been able to agree on anything for this weekend. We can try again at the next meeting."

"Hey, wait! Does that mean we aren't doing anything as a family this weekend?" chimes in Collin's sister.

"Yes, we need everyone to agree, and that is not happening," says the chairperson.

Now, things could go one of three ways:

1. The siblings will get on board with the paint ball idea (and no doubt have fun, in which case we can thank Collin at the next meeting for his great idea and insistence).

2. They will do nothing, and Collin will see that he is indeed important, and that people really do care about him, his thoughts and his preferences. He learns he will not be overruled or discounted. That feels good! His siblings might even work harder during the week not to pick on him so much, since they want his co-operation at the next family meeting. Things are looking up all-around for Collin.

3. Or, Collin might change his mind and agree to the wave pool. Wow, Collin, thanks so much for being willing to help the family this way!

The family meeting not only helped with planning the family fun, but by understanding Collin's goals and mistaken beliefs, the parents were able to use the family meeting as a way to show Collin experientially that he is loved and valued. Powerful stuff, isn't it?

USING THE FAMILY MEETING FOR THE ASSUMED INADEQUATE CHILD

Children who are so discouraged that their goal is to avoid may not want to attend the meeting. Remember, these children need to be shown just the smallest steps towards success. With these kids in the family, it is best to stay in Stage One until they join. Stage One meetings are fun, low-threat meetings. Invite them to the meeting and ask them if they would keep you company, even if they don't want to participate. It's a small, safe step that says they are important.

Also, beef up the acknowledgment portion of your meeting. Your deeply discouraged child needs to hear positives from each parent and from her siblings every week. If the deeply discouraged child offers up an appreciation for someone else, let her know how much her comment made an impact.

Try to draw forward the discouraged child by highlighting her strengths. "We're trying to plan our family fun for this weekend, and I was thinking of suggesting the park. Do you remember the last time we went and Julie was like the Pied Piper? All those little kids really wanted to play "What time is it, Mr. Wolf?" with you. You must have had 10 kids that you got into that game!"

The process may go more slowly when you are starting with a child who has the mistaken goal of assumed inadequacy, but week by week, these strategies will begin to repair and heal, and your family meetings can and will become more robust in time.

FROM BAD TO BETTER!

Are you nervous now? Don't be! Your meetings are going to go just fine. In fact, you are more ready than you know. You will learn along the way, and the best part about family meetings is that any problems you have in the meeting just become agenda items for everyone to solve together. People interrupting no longer has to be something that you alone must resolve. Now you can put it out there: "We need to discuss how to handle people interrupting each other at our family meetings. How can we do that better?" Or, "It seems to me that people use a lot of put-downs in the family meeting; how can we address that problem in our family?" I love family meetings because I don't have to be the brilliant one all the time. Share the load! It works better if you do.

You have learned so much about your children and probably something about yourself over the course of this book. You have the benefit of seeing your children for the wonderfully creative and resourceful people that they are. I hope your attitude about misbehavior is forever altered by the knowledge that our children are seekers. They are on a mission to fulfill their needs. How great is that? Our only enemy is discouragement. Remember, a growing ability to be encouraging and to help our children find their need for significance and belonging is now in your grasp.

There is no way for things not to improve over time as your family gels together and builds the bonds that will sustain you all. It's a change in the tides. With each improved skill, your children will shed more discouragement and begin to shine. Shifting from a punishment-and-reward model of parenting to a democratic model that is brimming with respect will bring about better behaviors and less need for correction of any kind.

We all know that success begets success, and you have already begun. Even applying just a few of the tools you have learned will bear results that will encourage you to keep on. You may re-visit this book often as you begin to apply what you have learned. You can also visit my website www.alyson.ca for ideas and tips on how to approach new situations that might arise. Join the other parents there that are also working to change their families for the better. We're building a community of support so you don't have to feel you're alone. Post comments, ask questions and find resources as you need them.

Parenting is a journey and it's a joy to know that I can be on that trek with you. Your children have everything to gain from your willingness to try something new, to keep on trying, even in the face of those "bad days" and setbacks. And they'll repay you for your efforts by being the most awesome next generation of people. They will become people who know how to get along, who know how to solve the problems of a global world that is filled with so much disparity. Your children will make a difference, because you parented them differently!